ELLEN BUXTON'S JOURNAL
1860 — 1864

Janet & Effie
threading beads

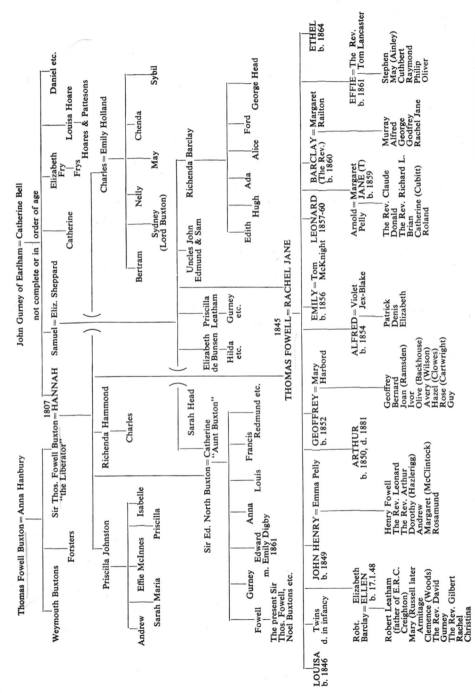

Thomas Fowell Buxton = Anna Hanbury

John Gurney of Earlham = Catherine Bell

not complete or in | order of age

Weymouth Buxtons

Sir Thos. Fowell Buxton = HANNAH (1807)
"the Liberator"

Samuel = Eliz. Sheppard

Elizabeth Fry — Frys, Hoares & Pattesons

Louisa Hoare

Daniel etc.

Priscilla Johnston

Forsters

Andrew — Sarah Maria
Effie McInnes
Isabelle — Priscilla

Richenda Hammond — Charles

Sir Ed. North Buxton = Catherine "Aunt Buxton"

Sarah Head

Francis — Redmund etc.

Gurney — Fowell, The present Sir Thos. Fowell, Noel Buxtons etc.

Edward m. Emily Digby 1861

Anna — Louis

Charles = Emily Holland

Catherine

Bertram
Sydney (Lord Buxton)
Nelly
May
Chenda

Richenda Barclay

Edith
Hugh
Ada
Alice
Ford
George Head

Uncles John Edmund & Sam

Elizabeth de Bunsen — Hilda etc.
Priscilla Leatham
Gurney etc.

THOMAS FOWELL = RACHEL JANE (1845)

GEOFFREY = Mary Harbord (b. 1852)

ARTHUR (b. 1850, d. 1881)

Geoffrey
Bernard
Ivor
Joan (Ramsden)
Olive (Backhouse)
Avery (Wilson)
Hazel (Clowes)
Rose (Cartwright)
Guy

ALFRED = Violet Jex-Blake (b. 1854)

Patrick
Denis
Elizabeth

EMILY = Tom McKnight (b. 1856)

LEONARD 1857-60

Arnold = Margaret JANE (T) Pelly (b. 1859)

The Rev. Claude
Donald
The Rev. Richard L.
Brian
Catherine (Cubitt)
Roland

BARCLAY = Margaret (The Rev.) Railton (b. 1860)

Murray
Alfred
George
Godfrey
Rachel Jane

EFFIE = The Rev. Tom Lancaster (b. 1861)

Stephen
May (Ainley)
Cuthbert
Raymond
Philip
Oliver

ETHEL (b. 1864)

LOUISA (b. 1846)

JOHN HENRY = Emma Pelly (b. 1849)

Twins d. in infancy

Robt. Barclay — Elizabeth = ELLEN (b. 17.1.48)

Robert Leatham (father of E.R.C. Creighton)
Mary (Russell later Armitage
Clemence (Woods)
The Rev. David
Gurney
Rachel
Christina

Henry Fowell
The Rev. Leonard
The Rev. Arthur
Dorothy (Hazlerigg)
Andrew
Margaret (McClintock)
Rosamund

THIS TREE ENDEAVOURS TO SHOW THE RELATIONS MENTIONED IN THE JOURNAL AND THE CHILDREN OF THE BUXTON CHILDREN

ELLEN BUXTON'S JOURNAL
1860 — 1864

ARRANGED BY HER GRAND-DAUGHTER

ELLEN R. C. CREIGHTON

PUBLISHED BY

GEOFFREY BLES . LONDON

SBN: 7138 0182 4

Printed in Great Britain
by Lowe & Brydone (Printers) Ltd., London

Published by
GEOFFREY BLES LTD.
52 Doughty Street, London, W.C.1
33 York Street, Sydney
531 Little Collins Street, Melbourne
70–2 Eagle Street, Brisbane
CML Building, King William Street, Adelaide
Lake Road, Northcote, Auckland
100 Lesmill Road, Don Mills, Ontario
P.O. Box 8879, Johannesburg
P.O. Box 834, Cape Town
P.O. Box 2800, Salisbury, Rhodesia

Contents

Guide to some other names not in the family tree

Barclay	(1) Ellen's youngest Gurney aunt married H. F. Barclay. The family lived near the Buxtons at Walthamstow. (2) Ellen's youngest brother was given Barclay as a christian name. (3) Ellen married Robert Barclay, a distant cousin, in 1868, so she is remembered as Mrs. Barclay.
Barnett	the coachman.
Carlos	a Patteson cousin.

Miss Chapman, Mr. Cotton; Mrs. Cooper, Brown, Pierce, Turner—inhabitants of Leytonstone.

Colin	the dog.
Derrogu or Derry	primarily a West African visitor but, after him, a very much loved naughty little black pony.
Cousin Edward	The Rev. E. Hoare, Rector of Aylesham, a notable evangelical preacher.
Eleanor, Emma	nursemaids.
Mr. Fitch	Vicar of Cromer
Foxwarren	Uncle Charles home near Leatherhead.
Frankie	a Patteson cousin.
Ham House	had been the home of Ellen's grandfather, Samuel Gurney; at the time of the journals the widowed Aunt Buxton and family were living there; demolished in 1872; the park is now West Ham Park.
Hanburys	related, and also connected in the brewing business.
Hemsworth	where the Leathams lived near Leeds.
Larry	T. F. B. the Liberator's gamekeeper and family friend; lived at Runton near Cromer.
Lisa	Louisa, Ellen's less lively, rather delicate elder sister.
Lucy and Martha	maids.
Marsden	the gardener.
Northrepps Hall	the home of Ellen's grandmother Buxton near Cromer.
Patteson	Vicar of Spitalfields, related through Hoares.
Rickerby	where Aunt and Uncle Head lived near Carlisle.
Ruth and Sarah	maids.
Miss Smith	the governess.
Taffy	nickname for Alfred.
Timmie	nickname for Emily.
Warlies	the home of Ellen's cousin, Sir Fowell Buxton, who married Lady Victoria Noel in 1862.

THE FRONT OF OUR OWN HOUSE FROM THE ROAD

Introduction

ELLEN BUXTON was the second of a large family of children living in the middle of the nineteenth century at Leytonstone, then outside London, by Wanstead Flats and just south of Epping Forest. They had a large Georgian House (now built round and used as a hospital) with a garden and a paddock for their ponies. Their father worked at the family brewery in Spitalfields; but they used to go for several months of the year to stay with their grandmother at Northrepps, near Cromer. Both there and round Leytonstone they had innumerable cousins, Buxtons, Gurneys, Barclays, Hoares, much intermarried, whose background was almost entirely Quaker; three consecutive generations of Buxtons had married Friends, though they themselves remained evangelical church people. Their life was permeated by their religion and the philanthropy arising from it; Ellen's grandfather (known in the family as the Liberator) was the leader of the campaign which led to the abolition of slavery; her grandmother was one of the Gurneys of Earlham, a sister of Elizabeth Fry, the prison reformer.

It is fortunate for us that Ellen had the enterprise and leisure to draw a great many sketches of her family, of the places they went to and of the

7

flowers they found, and besides this, between the ages of eleven and seventeen with few intermissions, to keep a journal, written up most days, in three fat ruled volumes in a large but closely-written hand. This diary was a record of the family's doings, not a receptacle for her private thoughts and feelings; it almost seems as if it did not occur to her to have any, and as if they were such a good united happy family that they had no quarrels and personal resentments. Nor do we ever hear of their being punished or repressed by those stern Victorian parents we have come to expect; but so much that can be called Victorian is there—an all-embracing religion with family prayers, Bible meetings, missionary activities and other good works; wealth from business, and the division between rich and poor taken for granted; a taste for sights and scenery, ruins, and railway journeys; for curios, wild flowers, and the Royal Family; a passion for little girls (*Alice in Wonderland* came out in 1866), always preferred to boys each time a birth is mentioned, an unquestioning sense of security; yet an unaffected familiarity with death—all this straight from the pen of a young girl in the middle of it, with great powers of enjoyment and creative ability and no critical sophistication to dull them.

This is the journal which I have abridged in this book, with illustrations from the sketch-books, most of them done on the spot, of things mentioned in the journal, but a few from later years, when Ellen sketched so well and left off writing in her diary. I have chosen the extracts to make a consecutive account of the children's life, so that we can get to know them and follow them through the four and a half years, while including anything amusing on its own account or characteristic of the time. Ellen lets us in to their life so vividly that I have left her to tell her own story, spelling and punctuation included, with as few notes as possible, and only one or two small transpositions of dates or incidents for smoothness' sake, and some substitutions of "we" for the endless lists of who did what and who rode whom; and to avoid frequent brackets and long explanations I have provided a family tree and a key of people and places requiring explanation. The sketches have been considerably reduced from their original size.

I should like to thank my cousin John Barclay for the loan of the diaries, and my uncles, aunt and cousins who have helped me with information, and Andrew Graham for advice.

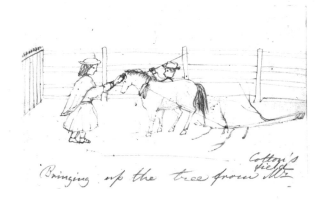

Bringing up the tree from Cotton's field

1860

Ellen kept a journal for part of 1859, but did not start in earnest until her twelfth birthday. Some extracts from 1860 give a picture of the sort of life the children lead.

17th January 1860 My Birthday   This morning Alfred and I took Mrs. Turner some sticks Mrs. Marsden gave us a beautiful Brown and white rabit, Mamma sent me a penwiper by the post, at twelve we dug up our gardens and in the afternoon we got a house for the rabit. In the evening we hid up little penny toys for the little ones then we had tea and a very pretty pink cake then we read till bed time.

Wednesday 18   This morning we dug up our gardens we gave Johnny and Arty each a kitchen garden, at four o'clock Johnney Arty and Me, went to Miss Chapmanns to tea First we had a dance then we had a christmas tree I had a little piano dancer Johnney a knife and Arty a puff-ball, they were very pretty indeed then we had a dance and then we came home.

Thursday 19   This morning Alfred and I staid in to paint, and at 12 we rode in the field. After dinner Miss Smith & the little ones went in a carriage for a drive to Chigwell.

Friday 20   This morning we stayed in because it rained Madmoiselle did not come in the afternoon Miss Smith Alfred and I went down the village we took Mrs Cooper some pudding and Mrs Brown some sticks, then we came in & played games till lesson time, in the evening we finished "Canadian Crusoes"

Saturday   This morning it rained very hard so we stayed in and made a house for the cats one of the crocuses came out today—in the afternoon we took some pudding to Mrs Cooper then Arty Geof and Alfred went in the pony chair with Miss Smith to Ham House and there they bought Alfred a bible, while Johnney and I stayed at home and made little cakes & biscuits. Today we bagan "The desert home". Mr. Taylor is come to spend the sunday he is a black missionary.

Sunday   This morning we went to Walthamstow church there was a sermon for the London Hospital they got 31 pounds Johnney found four eggs that his chickens had laid.

Monday   This morning we went to the bottom of the garden and helped Marsden to cut down an oak tree. It was not down till 4 o'clock. A french girl called Marie is come to stay with us she came and helped us cut down the tree.

Wednesday   This morning Papa did not got to London so we dug up a quantity of currant bushes to make a chicken yard, in the afternoon we had Shag's carriage and cut down a tree.

Thursday   This morning we helped Marsden to build the chicken house we put the gravel down and rolled it, and in the afternoon we tared the paillings of the chicken house.

Friday   This morning we painted the chicken house grey but afterwards it is to be green, and then we took some wood to Mrs Turner in the afternoon we all went with Derry to Lovewells but Lisa went to London with Mamma to see Doctor Kidd, I bought Lisa a little pocket book Arty a little pencil case and Geof a pair of scissors.

Monday This morning Alfred and I took Mrs Cooper a new testament and then we put the rabbit into the chicken house for he is to live there in the afternoon Aunt Sarah and Uncle Head came to see us, and then we rode in the field—

'LEYTONSTONE CHURCH FROM THE HAYFIELD'

Tuesday   This morning we took the rabit a walk in the garden he liked it
very much and then we tied Derry and Shag to a holly tree and made them
pull it down.

Feb 9   This morning we took a piece of carpet to Mrs Cooper and some
wood.   In the afternoon Mamma and I went in the carriage to London.
I took my work which was a very pretty peice of worstedd work for a bag.
I have just finished a very pretty little blue frock for dear Emily which
is braded with white braid.   Papa & I walked to 10 Upper Grosvenor Street
as we were going we went to the Baker Street bassar there were a great many
pretty things when we got there we found all the West End Missionarys
there to tea we all had tea with them and afterwards we had a sort of com-
mitee a great many of the missionarys spoke. *Sunday* . . . . after meeting
Papa and Uncle Sam went to one of the services for the people of the theatre.
Friday This morning we went to buy a bulfinch at the Pantheon.

The boys working in the garden

March 1.　This morning we went and bought seeds for our garden and we found the poor rabbit quite dead we dont know how he died in the afternoon we dug up our gardens and put in the seeds and potatoes.

Thursday　This afternoon Arty and Johnney Geof Marie Alfred and I had a ride in the field without saddles; I am learning to ride on the wrong side—

Saturday　This afternoon all Johnney's school fellows came and Francis and Doctor came and we had a rat hunt Aunt Barclay came and helped.

Saturday, 24　This morning we stayed in the garden and in the afternoon Papa took Johnney Arty and Geof to the "Basin" in Wanstead Park to fish Alfred and I followed on Derry and Princess we caught no fish because it was so cold but Alfred and I found 6 beautiful sprouting chestnuts which we planted today 8 chickens were hatched they were bantams and very pretty we put them in the hot house but one died.

Wednesday 28　Today is Alfreds birthday Papa gave him a book Lisa a prayer book Geof a money box & me a saw &c—after dinner we all blew bubbles—Edie Ada and Alice came to dinner they gave Alfred a book called "Rana" and a hoop then we all went a ride Johnney rode Franca, Arty Princess, Geof Derry, me Comet and Alfred Cowslip—as we were going over a very broad ditch full of water Cowslip put down his head to

Alfred tumbling into "Tathis Ditch" March 186

drink and Alfred rolled over his head into the water he got very wet indeed and we had to put him into the carriage (which was going) to go home and get dry—but as we were putting him in Comet laid down and rolled with me I had to get off because when he got up he began to kick and rear so I rode Cowslip and Comet ran after us, when we got home we all cut down a holly tree at the bottom of the garden, we had a very grand tea and cake—

Thursday 29   This afternoon Miss Smith Alfred and I went down the village to spend Alfred's half crown (that Aunt Barclay had given him) in tea and sugar for Mrs Pierce when we came back we chopped up the holly tree that we had cut down on Alfreds birthday—

Wednesday 11 April 1860   This morning Papa Mamma Lisa Johnney Arty Geof Alfred and I went to see the crystal Palace we first went all over the garden and then we went in, there was a concert there, we first had a sort of dinner then we went all over it and saw the great tree the birds the French court &c, &c, &c.   I bought a little vase for violets and a needlebook and Lisa bought a pencilcase and a knife for her pocket.

*There is now a gap of five months in the diary
during which Barclay was born.*

*   *   *   *   *

Sept 23 Sunday, Cromer.
Miss Smith Lisa Johnney Arthur Geoffrey Alfred & Myself came to Cromer
on the elventh of September.
This afternoon Barclay was baptised in Northrepps Church by Cousin
Edward Hoare, there was not nearly room in Grandmama's pew, so we had
to go to a great many other pews after the service we all went near the font;
he was very good indeed & hardly cried at all.
As we walked home we found that there were 30 of our *own* family & 40
counting the servants.

27th   Today there was a cricket match between the residents and the
visitors. Alfred & I went & sketched Cromer, in the afternoon some stopped
to see the match & the others went onto the shore & built fortifications.
They found quantities of agates on the shore.

Oct 1st   Papa took us a ride onto the lighthouse hills & there we found
quantities of other people on horseback, they practised for the sham fight
that is to be on friday, they practised again on Wednesday on the, shore.

Oct 5th   The Sham fight went off beautifully it was upon the lighthouse
hills there were 800 volunteers altogether, they came from Cromer Aylsham
& Norwich &c & they practised first upon the shore for a little while.
Uncle Charles looked so splendid on our Venice the only white horse & he
is in his uniform. There was there a horse without a tail.
The Voluntiers were divided into two divisions some were supposed to be
French & some English, they marched on the shore till they got beneath
the old lighthouse & the French drove the English up the cliff & then came
up themselves & then drove them to the new lighthouse, & they came into
the valley between the two lighthouses. Then the English charged the French
& made them run up the hill to the old lighthouse & down again on the way
to Cromer. Then they had another battle in Cousin Joseph Hoares field
& then they are supposed to have surrendered at discretion. I forgot to say
the cavalry looked the prettiest part of it, Papa was amongst them they wore

14

Cromer from the lighthouse hills. Sept 10 1862

red scarffs across their shouldiers & red ribbons in their hats. In the evening they made speeches & had fireworks & then late in the evening they had another engagement in boats.

15th   Arthur Geoffrey Alfred and I went to the reed house, & then we built a house of dead ferns & sticks it was nice and strong and we 6 could all go into it at once as we found out the next day.

The next day I had a letter from Edith to say my rabbit had two young ones but they are both black but on Saturday I had another letter to say they are both dead.

For the next few weeks I forgot to write my journal but we did nothing particular, we had rides, went out blackberrying &c &c, and came up (when Uncle Charles went away) from Cromer to stay at Northrepps.

Nov 20   Papa took us all in his Pheaton to see the hills at Runton, we took spades & dug up ferns &c, then we came to Larry's cottage and dug up a very large fern, which I am going to take home.

22 Nov   Papa and Mamma Grandmamma went away very comfortably this morning & when they were gone we had to get everything ready for our journey. I had my fern nicely packed up, & we had a hamper of prim-roses to take home with us, as well as some ducks and chickens four horses 6 ponies one carriage & one poney chair.

Nov 23   This morning we had breakfast at 7 o'clock, and Miss Smith, Arthur Geoffrey Alfred and Myself, started at 20 minutes to eight in our open carriage; Lisa Eleanor Martha Emily Leo and Janet waited for the coach. When we were in the carriage we watched the sun rise, it was very pleasant but rather cold, when we got near Aylsham we met the ponies; We did not stop at Aylsham but went right through with the horses on to Norwich where we met Mr. Gooch Miss Smiths brother-in-law. Soon after we had arrived, the coach came in with the babies, and Lisa, Janet was rather cross, and so was Leo, when he started, because Eleanor would not let him have a hole egg for breakfast. At 11o'clock we got into the train, Miss Smith Lisa Arthur Geoffrey Alfred & Myself went in one carriage and all the others went in one just behind it.
At 12 o'clock we in the first carriage had our luncheon, and at Ipswich Geof got into the other carriage and Timmie came into ours.
Arthur and I sent Geof messages by tieing a peice of paper to some string and letting it fly past his window when he would catch it, and write on the answer. We got out at Illford and found Aunt Barclay's carriage waiting for us. Colin came in the same train as we did and so did the ducks and chickens but the horses and carriages waited for the next train to rest themselves.
When we got home we found tea nearly ready, it was very pleasant to get home we went round and saw all the animals and then came in to tea. Derry came to us directly we called him. The nursery and Miss Smith's room have both been papered, and nearly all the house painted. We found quantities of Punches and illustrated London News to be looked at, which employed us for the rest of the evening.

Christmas Day 1860   We took a walk on to the forest with Shag's carriage, and Papa and Mamma Aunt Barclay Edith &c. came too, we went to the flats to meet the boys &c from Ham House but did not see them, in the evening Aunt Buxton Fowell Gurney Edward Redmund Louis and Francis all came to tea at seven and afterwards to hear the pieces we had learnt for Christmas, Louisa said "Cooper's mothers picture" I said "The Battle of the Lake Regillus", Johnney said "The mighty Hellvelyn" Arthur part of "Horatius" Geoffrey "Cassabeanca the heroic boy" and Alfred "Wreck of the Royal George"—we said them very nicely, in the evening we danced

16

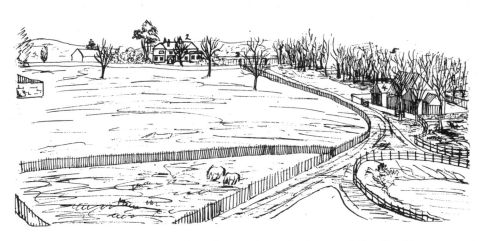

View from my window.

2 Mr. S[?]'s House.
3 Wanstead Park Pond.
4 Archery House.
5 Forest.

&c. till 9. I forgot to say a few days before Christmas Miss Smith went out for her holiday. She came home about three weeks afterwards.
Ever since the middle of December there has been capital skating we went nearly every day to Wanstead pond to skate.

1861

January 17 My birthday   Papa gave me a beautiful present of two books of British Moths, with beautiful painted pictures in it. Mamma gave me a beautiful paint box such a beauty.

Leo's death

Feb 4 Lisa's birthday   Poor little Leo died this morning at 4 o'clock, he had been ill since thursday morning. I will give a description of it:—

On Saturday, Jan. 26th, we took Leo to Ham House to see Aunt Buxton, with Papa, Mamma, Lisa and I, and the boys, we went on the ice poor little Leo tumbled down and cried but I do not think he hurt himself much, he got onto a chair and I pushed him about for a long time. That morning poor little Timmie was getting down off her chair when she fell over a can of boiling water and scalded her hands and knee dreadfully so she was put to bed she was very bright all day playing with baby &c, for she said her hands and knees did not hurt her much, except when the cotton wool and oil was put on fresh.

Sunday 27   Dear Leo quite well except looking very white as he always did Timmie quite happy in her little bed on the Bow room; Leo went out for a walk in the garden with us before church as usual.

Monday 28th   This morning Timmie seemed very dull and low indeed, she would not eat nor play. But dear Leo was quite well. In the afternoon we took Leo with us a walk to Aunt Barclay's we took Derry without a saddle for him to ride: when we got to the gravel pits we left Arthur Geoffrey and Alfred to try and catch lizards in the little ponds while Leo Lisa Papa Mamma and Myself went on to Aunt Barclay Leo rode Derry almost all the way there; how little we thought he would never take a ride again! . . . . When we got to Aunt Barclays we found Mrs Carter and Mrs Harrison there with their babies they admired Leo so very much and called him "like a little Angel" he was very much pleased with the beautiful blue and white hyrsenths. As we came home Leo complaining of being tired and rather cold when we got in he had forgotten to take off his galoshes in the hall so when he got to the stairs he sat down and said to Lisa "you can pull them off because they are not very dirty."

Tuesday   Leo came down this morning to reading and sat by Papa on the sofa he look so lovely by him with his very pale face Timmie is still very poorly, she looks feverish and is very low indeed. In the afternoon Leo went out into the garden and he was sorry to see all the Barley for the chickens spilt upon the ground so he stayed for a long time picking them up.

Wednesday   Leo quite well. Timmie still very poorly and wont eat any meat and hardly anything else but we are allowed to go in and see her: Saturday is her birthday but I am afraid she will have to spend it in bed poor little thing. In the afternoon Leo went out of doors Miss Smith met him and Sarah and Janet at the pond watching the boys skating and sliding, Miss Smith went on but Leo called out to her to stop for him. She took him with her and as they were coming round the garden he found a stick which he said would do for some poor woman.

Jan 31   This morning Leo had a bad earache he had had it all night and cried a great deal with it, he did not look at all well, poor little boy, but we did not think it was anything.
After breakfast Doctor Ansle came we had all been in to see Timmie that morning, he told us that she had the Scarlet Tina, but only slightly: and then we were quite sure that she had had it all Wednesday.
Dr. Ansle told us that dear Leo had it also but so very slightly; he had only a little rash under his arms and legs.
That morning at ten o'clock (before Dr Ansle had come) dear Leo had been sitting with us while we were at lessons and bible reading we gave him a pencil and paper to draw, he drew very nicely and when Lucy brought Arty and I our Codliver oil she said she would go and get dear Leo some orange for him to eat while he drew; which he enjoyed very much he looked very pale indeed, all over his face except one little spot on his right cheek which was very red.

Friday Feb 1st   This morning Leo was not very ill, neither was Mamma at all anxious about him, but Emily was much worse than he was, he had hardly any rash. At dinner time Papa took up Emily a choice peice of pheasant with breadsauce and potatoe, but she refused the pheasant and would only eat the breadsauce and potatoe, so Papa took it in to dear Leo which he ate ravenously, it was the last thing he ate that he enjoyed.

Saturday   Today is dear Emily's sixth birthday Leo rather worse he has very bad swellings on his glands and very little rash; in the afternoon he got much worse he could not swallow and hardly spoke and Mamma says he was in great pain till he died. In the evening she began to be quite anxious about him. Emily is much the same, though she is very ill.

Sunday   Dear Leo very ill indeed Mamma and Papa are very anxious about him; Emily is not so very ill but she will not eat anything. Aunt and Uncle Barclay came on their way to meeting and Papa told them how ill dear Leo was. We did not go to church at all for fear of infection.

Monday Feb 4   This morning when we went in to Mamma she told us that dear Leo had died in the night; we were all very sorry indeed she told us had died about 4 o'clock in the morning, and that had been in great pain before. We all stayed with Papa and Mamma till reading time in their room, then we went down to prayers and Papa read the first part of the XVIIIth chapter of Matthew with the text in it "There angels do always behold the face of my Father". After breakfast Aunt Buxton came and talked with Mamma and Papa, we settled with Miss Smith as usual at 10 o'clock but we did not do regular lessons, Lisa and I went to be with Mamma part of the time, to walk in the garden with her and Aunt Buxton.

6th   This morning Mamma told us that she wanted us to go and see dear Leo before he was put into his little coffin; Lisa Johnney and I went with Papa and Mamma after breakfast; he was lying in the large bed, and he looked so beautiful and so perfectly at rest; but he did not look at all like himself when he was alive, he was so changed I should not have known him I am sure and so exactly like Papa he looked much older than he really was, and so very handsome, his lips were very dark purple nearly black, and he had a sort of yellowish hue all over his face; his hands were under the sheets so we did not see them, there was a handkerchief tied round his face because Mamma said that it wanted support:
Papa told us to remember his dear face all our life & to look at him intently he did indeed look lovely, and just as though he were asleep; because his beautiful large brown eyes were shut.

Feb 7   Today is dear Leo's funeral; Cousin John Paterson is coming to bury him. There are to be a great many people all the Aunts and Uncles and cousins near are coming. . . . Cousin John Paterson came first, and we had a little walk in the garden when about eleven o'clock quantities of people came;

At 12 o'clock we began to walk to the churchyard Mamma and Papa went first then came Lisa and I, and then followed all the others, we first went to the churchyard where Cousin John Paterson met us reading some beautiful texts we then went into the church where we read some part of the service, then we went to the little corner in which the grave was dug, by the side of the little twins and Aunt Buxton's little boy. Then we came away and

Papa reading the Times.

Eleanor & Baby (Barclay) March 14/61.

walked home, when we got home Aunt Barclay & everybody else that had come went to Aunt Barclay's & left us all alone.

Sunday Feb 10   Today Timmie is much better we hope she gets up and sits on a chair sometimes and makes candle-lighters for all the house.

Today at dinner Mamma told us that Mary the Kitchen maid also was ill and that she would send her to the same house as Sarah (*who had also gone down with Scarletina*) so in the afternoon Mamma sent for a cab and for

21

Pennyfeather's cart to take her bed &c, while she went in the cab. Before she went Mamma did not exactly know whether it was the scarletina but the nurse sent back to say that she thought it was.

Tuesday 27   Emily is ever so much better she can run and walk alone which she thinks very clever with her sore knees she is extremely happy all day long painting &c but we are not yet allowed to go near her for fear of infection. We are very busy indeed cutting down quantities of bushes and planting new ones, we have planted all the roses and are now planting quantities of bushes in the place of those that are taken away.

28th   Today we are going to look all over the brewery. . . . We started at 12 o'clock in the open carriage with Papa, we picked up Johnney at Mr Wrights and had a nice drive to London.

After dinner Papa took us to see the beer made, we saw the malt in an enormous sort of barrel mixed up with hot water, which was getting all the good out of the malt, then there was a thing above that went round and poured the water on as it went, just like a water cart; It was very hot in some places because of the steam, there were tremendous furnaces with red hot irons to consume the smoke, we also saw the place where a poor man had got *twirled* into the irons & had got hurt tremendously. Once we saw *quantities* of half made beer rushing out of a pipe from one large sort of basin to another first came a quantity of steam and then a *rush* of beer which was boiling hot . . .

Feb 29   Today at 11 o'clock Mr. Bates the music master came, just as I had finished my lesson Mamma came in & told me to follow her out of doors when I had done so Miss Smith told me that dear Emily was walking out in the garden of course I rushed out and found them all in the greenhouse with Emily too Mamma said we might go near her in the garden though we might not in the house. In the afternoon she came out again and had a ride all round the garden in the little green cart, she enjoyed the flowers so much and particularly the snowdrops and daisies, she liked looking at the chickens and white ducks and asked us if we ever gave them bread, which we never do now Dear Leo used *always* to take out some bread to the ducks. Janet and baby were out in the garden too Timmie liked having them with her again very much. The other day Papa was talking to Timmie about Dear Leo and after he had gone away, she said that she would so like to go to Heaven and see him there.

22

March 5   All the time the scarlet fever has been in the house Janet and
Barclay have been up in the Green Room, so I go in every morning to hold
Barclay while they wash and dress Janet, I have been quite a nursemaid every
morning for more than a month, because there is only Martha and Emma to
dress Johnney, Arty, Geof, Alfred, Janet & baby; then at half past seven
Mamma comes up to wash & dress baby he is so good always laughing Miss
Smith Johnney, Arty, Geof, and Taffy breakfast at 8, & Lisa and I get our
music done and go and sit with them working.   Lisa and I wait to have
breakfast with Papa and Mamma when we have about half done Janet &
baby come down & stay with us till 10 o'clock when we *all* go to lessons in
the dining room with Miss Smith, then Martha comes down and takes care

Barclay.
7 o'clock A.M.
Green Room

Janet
March
16
1861

of the little ones in the drawing room, they go up at 11 o'clock to go to bed.
We finish lessons at a quarter to one, and I go up and see if the little ones
are awake, sometimes I give baby his bottle, it is great fun for Janet plays
about and makes baby laugh so he will hardly take it. If it is fine and warm
Timmie and Janet go out in the garden & sometimes baby goes too. The
babies go in about 3 o'clock & the boys and Lisa & I stay out till 4 when
we go in to lessons with Miss Smith, at ½ past 5 we have tea & at 6 I go up to
see Mamma undress baby, at about a quarter past 6 I go down for Janet
and undress her while Mamma finishes baby, or sometimes I give baby
his bottle before Janet comes up, then I undress Janet she does look so

23

7 o'clock A.M. Alfred
dials and my room.

pretty in her petticoat. Whenever I have taken off her frock she runs away round the bed and then comes back again and makes me help her put *her* baby to bed, when she is undressed she gets onto my lap while Martha prepares the bottle and I take off her shoes and stockings, when that is finished if her bottle is not ready she begins to fret till it is, she is in a great hurry to get it and enjoys it very much.

7th   We set off to the forest I drove Derry & Janet sat by my side, we first went past the Archery house (see picture opposite page 00) & then turned right, past the tadpole pond and then out again onto the road, just as we were coming to the flats we heard a band coming along with some rifle Volunteers, so just at that minute Mamma sent Papa to hold Derry's head and the minute the drum began again Derry gave a bolt and reared tremendously but he could not get away Johnny left go of Derry and another man (I do not know who he was) took hold of Derry on the side that Papa was not, so the drum continuing to beat Derry got tremendously frightened, and although Papa was holding him down with all his might he reared and stood up on his hind legs for about a minute it looked as though he were going to tumble over backwards onto Janet and me, who were still in the cart, when

24

Barnet meddlitating
over the broken spring
of Shag's carriage.
April. 22. 1861.

the drum had got a little further off Derry got a little quieter but he still reared a good deal, so Papa called out for Janet & me to get out & a boy lugged Janet out. I got out somehow I dont know how, then we drove home but Janet was very cross all the way. When we got home we took a grain tub and put it into the pond and let the boys swim about in it, they very nearly went over several times but it was great fun seeing them.

Mar 8 At $\frac{1}{2}$ past 5 Mr Bail came, the drawing master, Janet was in the drawing room and was great fun, she entirely lost her baby and looked about every where, for it, with Miss Smith, but they could find it anywhere, so

Baby in her cradle
Janet giving her the
bottle. Mar. 16

at last she got Miss Smith to make her a baby of an anti-maccassie rolled up$\frac{1}{2}$ at last she began to think of her baby again and said "Papa baby" then she pointed up to Mr. Bail who happily did not see, and said "Papa" most rediculously calling Mr. Bail Papa, at last Papa came down who had got her baby, she was very pleased to see it again.

Mar 14   Papa went up to London this morning in the poney chair and Mamma, Timmie, and Johnney went in the carriage at half past 12, to London where they would get Papa and go with him on to Hastings in the train.
In the afternoon Arty Geof Taffy and Myself went in Derry to dig up blue-bells in the forest, while Miss Smith and Lisa went in the poney chair to see Sarah who is at Jane Ridgewells she is going to follow Mamma to Hastings on Saturday, and Mamma Papa and Johnney come home on that day.
We got a great many bluebells and went and planted them round dear Leo's grave I hope they will live there and grow nicely; in the evening the boys went out as they do very often when it is light enough but I do not.

Going to dig up blue bells roots
with Derry in Shaghs carriage.
1 Alfred. 2 Arty. 3 Ellen. 4 Geof.
March 14 /67

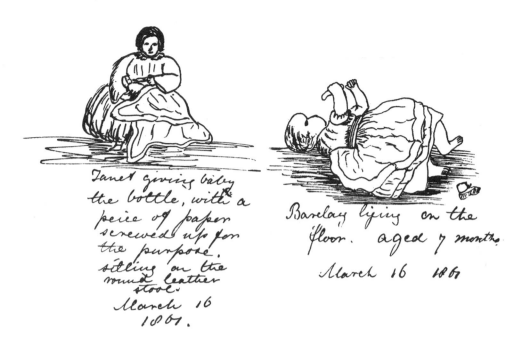

Janet giving baby the bottle, with a peice of paper screwed up for the purpose. sitting on the round leather stool. March 16 1861.

Barclay lying on the floor. aged 7 months. March 16 1861

Mar 15   I staid in the house with Janet she was very funny giving her baby the bottle with a piece of paper screwed up; and nursing it and putting it to bed &c. About 4 o'clock I went out with Miss Smith into the garden, we went to the greenhouse and picked some flowers for the drawing room, just as we were making them up Mamma Papa and Johnney came home from Hastings, Johnney had bought a beautiful ship which he took down directly to the pond to sail it sailed very nicely indeed. This morning there were two young chickens hatched though we did not expect them to hatch at all because the hen let them get cold 3 times, but there are some more eggs chipped so we hope to have some more tomorrow.
Yesterday the 5th volume of Macauley was published & it came to us today.

Sunday   This morning there were 8 chickens hatched out of ten, they are all black and very pretty, they are put in a coop in the tool house, with the rabit.

Monday   As we went to Ham House, Geof took Derry to the other side of a large ditch, and tried to make him jump it, he whipped him and Derry

27

reared but he would not go over it so at last Derry took geof into a holly bush as he always does when he is cross, and Geof whipped Derry and Derry kicked and Geof fell off but did not hurt himself in the least so Geof gave ip the fight and led Derry round.

In the evening Lisa Johnney and I went out to dinner with Mamma and Papa at Uncle Barclay's it was the first time we had ever been out to dinner. Afterwards we looked at two large portfolios one was all about the war in India, they were photographs, and were very interesting and pretty. We came home at 9 o'clock.

23 March   I have forgotten to say that all this time we have heard very good accounts of dear Barclay and Emily at Hastings, we hope to have them home on Friday.

April 24   I went with Papa Mamma, Lisa, Eleanor, Janet, Barclay and myself in the close carriage to London: we went to London to get Barclay and Janet pistolgraved and to take Lisa to Doctor Roth. When we got to the pistolgrave man (which was at 47 Baker St) we all got out; Janet and Baby had both had a very nice sleep in the carriage and Janet had become rather cross because coming out of the carriage had woke her up; so Papa carried her upstairs and Eleanor carried Barclay to a room where there were two men who had very large beards, and Janet was evidently very much afraid of men's beards because she screamed whenever they went near her.

*   *   *   *   *

June 2 . . .   We went to sketch in the forest, I sketched a very large Spanish chestnut and Arty a small one, it was the first time that Arty had ever sketched from nature.

June 21   This morning the hay in the meadow began to be cut and we all went down with Derry in his carriage to see it but it was so wet we could hardly play with it so at ten we came to the house and settled for lessons.

Today is Geof's birthday, but we are going to keep it till Monday or Tuesday as the hay is too wet to have tea in it, as we always have tea in the hay on Geof's birthday.

24th June   This morning a messenger came from the brewery with a note from Papa to Mamma to ask her to come up to London to see the remains of a dreadful fire that on Saturday night had burnt down a very large warehouse close to London Bridge. We were visiting some of the poor people in the Back lane, he very soon found us and we went home directly and Mamma, Alice and Phena Fry, Johnney, Arty, Geoffrey, Alfred and myself all drove up to London in the open carriage; first to the brewery where we found Papa and took him with us, then over London Bridge where we had a most beautiful view of the burnt warf, and the whole bridge was so crowded with carts and people, we could with great difficulty get along; but when at last we did get over the other side we hired a boat and went on the river to see the burning warehouse; for the fire was still burning upon the ground it looked just like an old ruin with no roofs and only walls left though it looked very beautiful.

June 28   This afternoon at four o'clock we rode to see Prince Albert laying the foundation stone of a new "Merchant Seaman's Orphan Asylum": Papa went to see the stone laid, with Uncle Barclay. So at four Johnney Geoff Taffy and I got onto our ponies and rode to Aunt Barclay's where we found Edith, Hugh, Ada and Alice going to ride with us, so we went directly to the Whipps Cross corner and there on the grass we drew up our ponies all in line and so waited for about a quarter of an hour, then at five minutes to five we saw all the people's heads turn towards London and Aunt Barclay called out to us that Prince Consort was coming first came two people on horseback then a carriage with four bay horses and postilions, in which was Prince Albert, with two gentlemen beside him, so when he saw all us eight children drawn up in a line on our ponies, and the boys took off their hats, he took off his hat to us, and Aunt Barclay heard and saw him say—"Oh how pretty"—, then he passed on and another carriage came with four grey horses with some more gentlemen in, then when they had all passed, we galloped as hard as we could home to Aunt Barclay's, and rode into the hay field and jumped over the long lines of hay and then went to one end of the field and galloped as hard as we could go to the other. . . .

July 24   Today the boys and I began to build a "church', and enclosed it with a wall as a burial ground and in it we buried five little ducks, and one little chicken, that had died, the church we built of bricks; and plaistered them together with mold and water, the steeple was about four feet high, and the church was about 2 feet; there were four windows on each side of the church and a door at the end, then we cut a very long tombstone to put all along the graves of the little ducks for they were all in a row, the tombstone was made of deal wood, first we white-washed it and then wrote "5 LITTLE DUCKS ONE CHICKEN" on it with Indian Ink.

July 25   To-day I went with Papa and the boys to fish at Carshalton . . . Arty and I walked a little up the river and saw quantities of enormous trout, and some sticklebats, so we stayed there and Arty and I fished for sticklebats

May 16
1865

fishing at Nun...ton
donkey   J.J.B

with Papa's landing net, which he had lent us; very soon we caught a
"Miller's Thumb" and then a sticklebat, and before dinner we had caught
five sticklebats.

31   This morning Aunt Barclay had 160 Bible women to entertain; and
in the afternoon at thee o'clock Miss Smith and Lisa went in the poney chair
to help and Johnney, Geof, Taffy and I rode there; we found Edith, Ada, and
Hugh riding in the little field where a large tent was put up for the Bible
women to have dinner and tea in; So we all went into the big field and
galloped about till about four, then we came indoors and at five the Bible
women all had their tea, and we went and helped hand the cups &c. round;
They seemed to enjoy themselves very much and at six Mr. Wilkins, and Capt.
Trotter adressed them till about seven o'clock when a great many carriages,
flys &c came and took away several ladies and gentlemen who had come to
see the bible women then ten vans came and took them all away and as they

Going through the river Lea
Aug. 23. 1861 —
2 Cowslip (following)
3 Johnney on Comet
4 Alfred on Princess
5 Papa on Delhi
6 Frankie Pateson on Franca
7 Geof on Derry
8 E.E.B on Garry —

passed through the gate to get into the vans, Edith and I stood at each side and gave each a little bunch of flowers, which they liked extremely.
Today Aunt Barclay was so deaf that everyone had to speak to her through a tube that she had on purpose.

Aug 13   After luncheon, we took, Eleanor, Sarah, Geof, Alfred, Timmie, Janet and Barclay, to have their pictures taken at a photographic van that had come to spend a fortnight on a flat peice of grass just opposite our gates, Janet, Timmie, Alfred and Baby were to have their pictures taken; so some of us went in but directly we got inside Janet did not like it and began to cry and roar very much, so we got a nice picture of baby on Eleanor's lap and one of Alfred; then we got Derry in his carriage, and, were photographed in it; it stood at the side of the road, and Timmie, Janet, Baby and I were inside, Alfred on the box, Geof holding Derry and Miss Smith by the side; the first one was a very good one all except that Barclay would not keep his head still and it came out just like a smudge, but all the rest was very good

indeed, then the man took another which was not so good.

In the afternoon at five o'clock we went to see Chingford church, when we got there we all got off tied our ponies up to the posts that were near; & got the tea out of the carriage; first we thought of having for our tea table, a large stone vault, and had laid the cloth all ready; but then we thought we had better not, so we took it & put it out in a field near, and there ate it, we had a very good tea for there were, lobster sandwiches, iced butter, roasted apples, plums and currants. When we had done tea, we looked all over the church though we could not go in it was all covered over with most beautiful ivy.

Aug 15   In the afternoon Papa, Johnney, Geof, Alfred, Frankie & I rode through the Lea and then galloped on the marshes we had great fun going through the Lea for Geof could hardly get through as Derry was so little he had to put up his legs quite high and let Derry go through as he could.

Friday, Aug 16   Barclay's birthday, one year old. Today we all had tea in the garden in honour of Barclay's birthday, and invited Louisa, Ada and Harry Fry, and all the Barclays to tea, Uncle Barclay gave Barclay a most beautiful silver mug with his name engraved on it, and a beautiful raised

c

picture of two boys on a sea-saw. He had a very nice little cake with quantities of sugar on it. After tea we got Shag in his carriage, and all the little children rode in that, and we all took a walk in the cornfields.

To Northrepps Again

Sept 5   This morning about eight o'clock we went into the stable yard and saw the carriage being packed with parcels &c. to go in the train; Garry, Franca and Princess, were caught also, and had their saddles and bridles on ready to go in the train, then the two carriage horses were put in the carriage and it drove off to the station with nobody but Barnet in it. George rode one of Papa's horses and led Garry and Franca, and let Princess run loose. At Stratford station the horses, ponies and carriage were put into the train. Then about nine o'clock a fly came to the door, and Eleanor, Sarah, Taffy, Timmie, Janet and Barclay were packed into it and drove off to Stratford Station. When they were all gone we turned out three of the horses in the field, and they kicked and ran about with Cowslip, Comet, Shag and Derry. In the afternoon we put neat everything and helped to pack up &c. &c.

Sept 6   This morning we were very busy, and had breakfast at eight, at nine the fly came for us, and Papa, Mamma, Lisa, Johnney, Geof and I got into it, and said good-bye to all the maids, and then drove off to Stratford station. There we got into the train and had a very nice journey to Norwich, we had a very nice luncheon on the train at about twelve and when we had finished we tied up some piece of bread &c. that we did not eat and tied them all up in paper parcels and then gave them away to some little boys. I worked and drew in the train and the others read. We took Bully to Northrepps in his cage, and he seemed to enjoy it, when we arrived at Norwich there was Grandmama's carriage all ready waiting for us, and as there was a postilion and post-horses, Papa, Johnney, Geof, and I went on the box, and Lisa and Mamma went inside. . . .

Thursday   This afternoon we all went to Beeston Bog to find wild flowers some of us rode there and the rest went in the carriage, when we got there we found the beautiful Grass of Parnassus growing all over the bog, and a great many other lovely flowers, we brought home a great many, some we did not know at all, and nearly all the flowers we found in Beeston bog were white.

34

Saturday   This morning the new donkey cart came home so we took a drive in it in the wood & picked some blackberries; it was a very nice green donkey cart with two seats.

Sunday   Grandmamma's birthday. aged 78. This morning we walked to Northrepps Church and Grandmamma and Mama came in the carriage. Mr. Law preached a sermon on the same text that he had preached upon two years before.
In the afternoon we had a nice sermon from a Mr. Govette about the jews and then we had a collection for the Jews. Grandmamma is seventy-eight today, she was born in the year 1783.

Thursday, Sept 19   Today it was a very fine day so a great many of us took our luncheon and had a picnic on the Runton Hills, which were all covered with bright purple heath, and rich brown ferns. A great many of us rode and all the rest came in four carriages and two or three poney-chairs—and altogether it was a very pretty sight with the riders in front and the carriages behind. When we got to the Runton Hills we got out and sent the carriages and horses to Larry's cottage, and we got into a very nice place on the purple hether and then we all spread out our luncheon, and first appeared an immense quantity of meat pies, then some cake, buns, bread, cheese, butter,

'A PICNIC ON RUNTON HILLS—SEPT. 19, 1861'

1. Mama
2. Papa
3. Uncle Charles
4. Aunt Emily
5. Johnney
6. Arty
7. Geof
8. Alfred
9. Sydney
10. Miss Smith
11. a Mr. Champness
12. another Mr. Champness
13. another Mr. Champness
14. a Miss Champness
15.
16. } Miss Warens
17.

18. Cousin Joseph Hoare
19. Cousin Gurney Hoare
20. Cousin Caroline Hoare
21. Cousin Juliana Hoare
22. Sam Hoare
23. Robin Hoare
24. Louisa
25. Emma Bunsen
26. little Karl Bunsen
27.
28. } Miss Harcourts
29. Miss Herring
30. Mr. Gedge
31. Miss Day

tartlets, beer and water, and we had a very nice luncheon, then I got up into an oak tree and sketched all the party.

Thursday   This morning we lighted a fire in Papa's sitting room, and then made some blackberry jam, from the blackberries we got yesterday and those from the Warren; there were more than five pounds of blackberries and we put them into a saucepan with plenty of sugar and boiled them for half and hour, then we poured them into eight pots, and Grandma came and tasted it and she said it was very good indeed.

Monday, Sept 30   . . . This evening at Stratford (near London) they opened a very handsome fountain in remembrance of Grandpapa Gurney; it is very near Stratford church and a very high pillar from the top of it: we suppose Aunt Buxton and Uncle Samuel went to the opening of it.

Wednesday, Oct 16   Today there was a volunteer review in Gunton Hall, they seemed to enjoy it very much and they had a very nice cold dinner, off bread, meat, plum puddings, Sherry, and beer they had a little bow of ribbon given them of grey & white ribbon, and on two strings was printed—
            "Assert Old England's Freedom" . . .

Oct 27th   All this month it has been very warm indeed for October, sometimes quite like summer.

There is such a charming new cockatoo here now, he is quite tame and very mischievous, he will come down to anybody here he sees in the garden and bite their legs or turn over on his back before them and talk, but very often he will come into the schoolroom while we are at lessons and will not go out again.

Wednesday, Oct 30   This afternoon Papa, Johnney, Arty, Geof, Alfred and I rode to Joys Mill on Rowton Heath, so we went into it and saw them grinding the corn, sifting it &c. altogether it was a very interesting sight, then we had a nice ride to some woods at Runton where we got off and picked ip a quantity of Spanish Chestnuts to eat.

Saturday, Nov 2   This morning for the first time this Autumn we had a Snow storm it was very cold indeed, but I lighted my candle at six o'clock as I do every day and sat up in my bed and worked: Lisa comes in and dresses with me—It rained very hard all day today and there was such a high wind—So in the afternoon Papa, Gurney, Andrew, Fowell, Johnney, Geof, Arty, Alfred and I took a walk onto the lighthouse hills, and there it was so tremendously windy, that sometimes we were nearly blown away twice I could not stop myself in the least and sometimes we sat down or else we knew we should not be able to standstill; it was well that we took Colin, Carol, and Carr, the three dogs or else we should all have lost our caps, but we had a very nice walk and all got ourselves very nice and warm, and then we came home to lessons and tea—

Monday, Nov 4   Miss Smith went off this morning by coach to Norwich to stay with her sister till Thursday she took with her our dear naughty, mischievous cockatoo, which is going to live with Miss Smith's sister.

Wednesday   We are very busy packing up today I pack up the lesson books as there is no Miss Smith, my bullfinch that I brought from Leytonstone was put into his own cage today, ready to go tomorrow morning early. Today Papa, Andrew and Geof went out fishing at Gunton and caught two big pike.

Thursday, Nov 7   When we arrived at Leytonstone we went into the garden and looked all about, and everything looked very nice indeed but there were no flowers except chrysanthemums.

38

'DEPARTURE BY COACH'

Nov 16   Timmie and Janet enjoy being home very much they went today and saw the chickens, rabbits, ducks, cows, dogs, calves and ponies. It is very cold ineed now, so in the morning nearly every day before lessons, we catch Derry, tie him to the green cart and make him drag it round the garden while fill it with sticks and when it is full we take it down the village to the poor people.

Tuesday, Nov 20   This morning Arty, Geof and Alfred went and skated on our pond for it bears very nicely, Johnney could not go because he goes every day at nine o'clock to his school.

Wednesday, Nov 21   All last night there was a thaw but Geof went onto the pond and skated and Arty and I put Derry into the green cart went down the village & bought a hundred weight of coals for sixteen pence, it was

Arty's own money, and he and I took them in the green cart to a very poor woman Mrs. Squires in the Cribb—then we went onto the ice with Geof, and came in to lessons at ten.

Papa has bought a whole ton of white carrots to give to the ponies when we like, we have some every year.

Barclay can walk all across the nursery now alone, he is getting on so nicely and can talk a little.

Thursday, Dec 5 (*The birth of Effie*)
Such a good piece of news for todays journal—
This morning Mama was not well she got up late had breakfast in the Maple Room—and staid there all the morning, she has not been at all well since Sunday. After luncheon, Mama went out in the garden a little, and then she went a drive in the carriage—
Aunt Buxton came and staid here all the evening and all night too—
Dr. Ansle also came and slept here—
In the evening just at half past eight Miss Smith, Lisa Johnney and I were sitting reading and talking in the drawing room when exactly at half past eight, Papa walked in and told us that we had a new baby, a little sister, of course we were all very much pleased, and when we were in bed Miss Smith came in and told us all about her—she is like Janet with a round face, but we cannot see what coloured eyes she has—Mama is getting on very nicely indeed.
. . . . On Friday morning I went in and saw her and the baby too—
The baby is delightful we have already fixed her name it is to be "Effie" which we all think is very pretty.

Monday, Dec 9   We have been today to see Uncle Barclays gutta percha works—Lisa, Johnney, Arty, Geof, Alfred and I went up in the carriage at ten o'clock to the brewery, when we arrived there, Papa got into the carriage with us, and we all drove together to the Gutta Percha works in Warf Road. Uncle Barclay was there all ready to take us to see it—he took us first down into the cellar and showed us the immense pieces of Gutta Percha then he showed us through the whole process, how it was first cut and mashed up, washed cleaned and done all kinds of things to it there was a great deal of machinery, much more than in the brewery, sometimes we got some little soft pieces and worked them up into little balls till they were hard—before

40

we went away Uncle Barclay gave each of the boys an Indian rubber ball he gave a gutta percha basket to Lisa and a little vase to me. Then Uncle Barclay drove home in his gig, and we behind him in our carriage.

Sunday, Dec 15 Death of the Prince Consort. The Prince Consort has been seriously ill for the last week with gastric fever, Papa sent down to get an evening paper last night to see if there was any news about him. . . . At church the Prince Consort's name was left out in the Litany so after church we asked the pew opener and she told us that he died last night at eleven o'clock.

Monday   The newspapers were all covered with black lines between each column. The funeral is to be at Windsor next Monday—
The Queen and her children are going to Osborne on Thursday—

Saturday   There is a great deal about the Queen and the dead Prince in the papers the chapel at Windsor is all being hung with black cloth—
Mama is getting on very nicely and the baby is such a charming little girl.
We are all going to ride today to register her at Walthamstow.
The chickens are very flourishing now they lay a great many eggs every day and while Johnney is out I take care of them.

Monday, Dec 23   This afternoon we went to the Alms houses near here and gave to each of the people half a pound of tea & a pound of sugar, which they liked very much.

Tuesday, Dec 24   Christmas Eve   This morning we got Shag's carriage and tied Derry into the green cart and then Papa and all the boys & I went around the garden to pick an immense quantity of holly and evergreens, to decorate the house with, so when we thought we had got enough we all set to work to make large wreaths &c, first we made two very long ones that we put twisting round the two large pillars in front of the house, and then we took large bunches of holly indoors and put it all about the hall, then we did the drawing room and the nursery till all the house was very pretty.

Wednesday, Dec 25: Christmas Day   Last night, we filled Timmie's, Alfred's, Janet's and Barclay's stockings with some little presents, and so when they went to put on their stockings this morning they found all the things and were very much pleased with them. We went to Church this

41

The Christmas dinner

morning at eleven and saw the Church all nicely decorated with evergreens. In the afternoon at two o'clock we all had a nice walk—now I am going to mention each person that walked with us—

Aunt Buxton, Fowell, Edward, Redmund, Louis, Francis, Anna, Eva, Aunt Barclay, Uncle Barclay, Edith, Hugh, Ada, Alice, Papa, Lisa Arty, Geof, Alfred and I.

We took a nice walk in the forest, and about four we all separated and went home.

On Christmas day in the evening Papa, Arthur, Lisa, Geoffrey & I went to say our Christmas peices at Aunt Barclays.

Every year we all of us learn a piece of poetry to say at Christmas, so this year we all went in the carriage and said them at Aunt Barclays, they were all very pretty peices & very nicely said, it took just an hour and a half to say them all. At half past six we had a beautiful dinner with two Turkies, because one was not enough, we also had a plum pudding on fire, After dinner we played games and went away about eight.

Dec. 28

This afternoon we all took a ride with the Barclay's onto the marshes near the Lea, we had great fun going through the river and then we rode on and saw how the immense sewer (which is being made through Stratford) crosses the Lea, in a sort of tunnel ten feet above the water.

Perhaps Mama is going downstairs tomorrow she is perfectly well now and wishes to be down.

I have now put in some pictures about the Prince Consort's funeral which took place on Monday, the 23rd.

1862

Wednesday, Jan 1st, 1862   This morning Lisa, Arty, Geof, Alfred and I went & opened the door of the room where Mama & Papa were sleeping & sung them a hymn without them seeing us then we went in and wished them a happy new year—this we generally do every Christmas day but Mama & Papa were not together this Christmas day, so we did it on New Years morning.

Thursday, 2   This afternoon Geof, Arty & I drove in tandem to Aunt Barclay's this time we had Shag for our leader & Derry in the shafts & we went much quicker than if we had put Derry in front.

Monday, Jan 6   This afternoon I went up to London to Daniel's in Bond Street to buy a wedding present for Edward & Emily who are to be married on the 23rd of January. We saw some lovely tea sets, & Papa chose one set which was most exquisite, it was painted all over with very beautiful fine peices of grass, and butterflies and other pretty insects, flying about upon the grass. . . . .

(2) Derry and (3) Shag, tandom, going to Aunt Barclay's
(4) Alfred. (5) E. C. D. (6) Arthur in (7) Shag's carriage.
Jan. 1862.

Friday, Jan 17th My Birthday   It is intensely cold now, and the ice on the ponds will bear beautifully, so this morning Arty, Alfred & I went and skated on our pond—

This afternoon we had the last dancing lesson, and when Edith Ada and Alice came to it they each brought me a very pretty birthday present, and in the evening Mama gave me a book called "Williss's Poetical Works". Miss Smith went away last Wednesday so we are having holidays. I am fourteen years old today.

Sunday, Feb 2   Today is Emily's birthday. Mama gave her a very pretty book for a birthday present & she had a beautiful cake covered with pink sugar at luncheon—In the afternoon she went to church for the first time, and she liked it very much—Last year on her birthday she was in bed very ill with scarlet fever, so was dear Leo., Timmie is 6 years old today.

Wednesday, Feb 5   That dear, good, sweet little Effie is to be christened tomorrow & tomorrow we are going to have the christmas tree—today we took a ride to see a most curious orkid which grows in Mr. Warner's greenhouse. It was most exquisite like a very large star and very rare. It was a plant from Madagascar.

Thursday, Feb 6 *Effie's Christening*
When the service began, we all stood round the font in a circle & Janet & Barclay stood upon the seat of one of the open pews in the aisle & behaved most improperly, they were very good at the beginning except that Barclay would kick against the back of the pew & make a noise, but Janet was quiet & good. Soon Barclay began to get tired of standing still, so he insisted upon getting down, and we were obliged to let him, because if we stoped him, he would begin to scream; then Janet insisted upon going after Barclay, and they two played together in amongst the open pews, but they did not make much noise and if we tried to stop them they would cry, so it was the best plan to leave them to do as they pleased. All this time the service was going on very nicely, Effie was perfectly good.

In the afternoon the boys had lessons early, and Lisa Miss Smith & I were putting the things on the Christmas tree, when several of the party came, but we finished ornamenting the tree & then I made some wreaths for Lisa, Emily & I to wear, and then ornamented the cake, which every one thought extremely pretty.

Picking primroses at Warlies

March 29 – 1862 –
1 Mama
2 Papa
3 Cousin Elizabeth Pateson
4 Edith –
5 Ada
6 Alice
7 Myself
8 Alfred
9 Arty
10 Timmie
11 Alice Pateson
12 Louisa –

After tea, we had our little magic lantern, which Uncle Sam gave to Lisa a long time ago, and it was very pretty, and great fun—then Uncle and Aunt Barclay came, and we lighted the tree, and then all went in, and we cut off the things & everybody had something and they were very much pleased with their presents—The schoolroom was quite crowded with people.

Friday, Mar 14   We went and bought some seeds in the village, & sowed them in our gardens, I have a great many things in my garden now, Peas, beans, potatoes, Radishes, Lettuces, Spinage, Brussels sprots, Cabbages, French beans, and Brocoli. This afternoon Johnney, Arty, Geoffrey, Alfred and I took a nice ride with Uncle Barclay, Edith, Ada and Alice first we went to Stratford & bought a thing of moss and hair for the canaries to build with.

Wednesday, Mar 26   Aunt Barclay's baby's name is to be "George Head" which we think is very ugly. When Uncle Barclay heard that he had got another son, the only thing he said was—"Hang him", because he was so sorry it was not a girl.

Saturday, Mar 29   This afternoon we all went to dig up primroses at Warlies. When we got there we took out the baskets trowels and hampers and carried them across wet grass and mud, to the wood where the primroses grow, when we got there they did look so lovely the ground was all covered with them, and we dug up a great quantity enough to fill both hampers, and picked whole baskets full, we could not find any birdnests, because it is too early I suppose. We staid in the wood about an hour, and then walked off to the carriage, and drove home.

As we went we ate some biscuits & milk, because we were very hungry. All Sunday the two hampers were standing outside the hall door, and they looked very beautiful, quite full of primroses.

April 2nd   Today Baby was put into short clothes she looks so pretty, I think much prettier than when she was in long clothes she has got the most beautiful little flannel petty coat I ever saw.

Papa sent two beautiful Ruff Legged Falcons to the Zoological Gardens, which had been caught by one of the gamekeepers in Norfolk so on Saturday we went to the Zoological Gardens to see them, and had a very pleasant day, and enjoyed ourselves extremely, and took some bread and gave it to the animals.

Effie in long clothes.

Effie in short Clothes.
April 5. 1862

On Thursday we went into the forest & got quantities of wood anemonies &
bluebell roots, the wood anemonies were fully out, and we picked a great
many and put them into a very pretty white thing for flowers in the antiroom.
On Friday we made Arthur a garden for wild flowers near the hot house &
planted some primroses, anemonies and bluebells in it—
I have got 8 young date trees that I grew from date stones last year & they
are growing nicely—I have also planted some orange pips to see if they will
grow, and two apricot trees and a cherry tree that I grew from stones last
year—My garden is going on so nicely, the things have all grown, and my
potatoes are up.

Easter Sunday, April 20   Yesterday we made some wreaths of primroses
& nosegays, to put into our three little graves in the church yard, so this
morning we took them, and put some flowers on each, & they all looked
very pretty, we always keep flowers growing there.
Lisa and I are going to be confirmed on the fourteenth of May next and I
hope that God will indeed prepare me for it by his Holy Spirit. We have twice
been to see Cousin John Paterson, and he has given us questions to answer
for him. This is the happiest day to me in all the year. I think the thought
of Christs Resurrection is so delightful.

On Easter Monday we took a nice ride into the forest, & saw primroses, wood anemonies, Stelaria, wild Strawberries, & dog violets all in blossom & the trees with their green foliage looked lovely.

Tuesday, April 22   It was a wet day so instead of having Easter eggs in the garden they were hidden all over the house & Aunt Barclay sat upon one— then there was a bran tub & we all got presents out of it, I got a lovely little shell made of biscuit china for flowers, & every body else had something nice. We had tea at six & then games till we went away at seven.

April 25   This morning the four boys & I went up to London in the train all alone to the Brewery. There we had luncheon, and then Papa and we went in a cab to see the Mint, when we got there a man took us to see the copper being coined, but there was no gold or silver being coined, which was very interesting. There was such *hosts* of old pennies & Papa says that the Brewery send the mint a hundred pounds worth of copper every day to be exchanged for new pence.
When we had seen the mint we went & saw all over the Tower of London, which was very interesting but we had seen it before.

April 26   Uncle Edmund turned out a whole herd of young pigs into the yard & said that whoever could catch one should have it, so Carlos caught one & Uncle Edmund gave it to him, then Papa bought it of Carlos to take home to Leytonstone as Carlos could not keep it at Spitalfields, so Papa gave him a pound for it.

'GOING INTO THE FOREST TO FIND WOOD ANEMONES—APRIL 7, 1862
2 JANET. 3 BARCLAY. 4 DERRY. 5 TIMMIE. 6 MYSELF'.

Tuesday, April 29   This afternoon Mr. Harrison got on very nicely with the picture he is making of Emily, Janet and Barclay and it is very pretty indeed—Mr. Harrison is such an odd man, he had tea in the nursery and dinner, and when he came from London he brought a hair brush & comb with him, to brush his dog every morning.

Our canaries are sitting on three eggs, only they are very stupid & when we gave them a hedge sparrows egg to sit upon as well as their own they wood not have it but kicked it out of the nest—We have had hot house strawberries for a long while now, they are so delicious.

On the first of May was opened by the Duke of Cambridge the Great Exhibition of 1862, and today we read all about it in the newspaper it seems to have gone off very prosperously but it was sad that Prince Albert could not have been there.

Monday, May 5   We have got five lovely nests in our garden now.

I have got a pair of summer skates which I like very much they go with four indian rubber wheels in the middle of the foot.

Friday, May 9   Today we all went to see the Bank of England, Mama, Papa, Johnnie, Arty, Alfred & I all started at twelve o'clock in the open carriage. Lisa did not come because she was tired but we had a long drive there, & when we got out we found Mr. Cotton (a kind gentleman, who shows the bank & lives near Leytonstone) all ready to take us to see every thing. First we went through a room, where we saw the state in which the silver comes over, then we went into the cellars & saw the gold, it was in square masses, each worth 700 pounds, & a whole truck full was worth 80,000 pounds, then we saw silver, in the same state, but larger blocks, in the cellar the gold show most beautifully, but the silver was dull. Then we went to a room which had very curious machines in it, invented by Mr. Cotton himself they were constructed so as to throw all the good sovereigns into one box, and all the old ones which were light into another box, we staid there a very long while for it was very curious to watch. Then they took all the old sovereigns out of the boxes & put them into a machine which cut a slit in them, so as to show they were bad, & then they were melted down again to make good sovereigns. . . .

Wednesday, May 14   Today was our Confirmation—It was at Woodford Church—Mama, Papa, Lisa & I were there at eleven o'clock but the Bishop

of London did not come till twelve—It was a most interesting service, & the Bishop gave us a beautiful sermon. There were four hundred candidates altogether. In the middle of the sermon a young lady that had come to see the Confirmation fainted, so she was carried to the parsonage where she soon after died.

Friday, May 16   This morning we went to see the horticultural Gardens near the International Exhibition, they were very pretty especially the immense Green House. In the afternoon we went to see the International Exhibition we thought it very grand, but I cannot tell all the things we saw, there were such lovely things, I never saw such silver in all my life we saw the largest diamond in the world & all kinds of other valuable stones, & all kinds of glass, furs, shawls, silks, wax fruit, busts & every imaginable thing, we saw the picture gallery, & staid there a very long time, there were principally foreign pictures & very beautiful.

There was the largest topaz, the largest emerald, the largest carbuncle, the largest ruby, the largest opearl, the largest diamond & the largest saphire in the world—But the silver plate was the thing I admired the most I think, and there was a great deal of it, & the glass also was very beautiful.

Wednesday, May 21   My Bulfinch is such a charming bird he gets on my head & sings & always knows me when I come into the room.

We have 8 ponies now in the field Canvass (the pony chair pony) Garibaldi, (my pony) Franca (Johnney's pony) Cowslip (Arties pony) Derry (Taffy's pony) Princess (Emily's Pony) Shag (the pony that goes in the little carriage) and the new grey pony.

Sunday, May 25   We had a nice drive in the open carriage to Plaistow meeting, and got there rather early; it was a very interesting meeting for a good many people preached, as it was the yearly meeting, it ended about half past twelve, & then all the Friends, nearly everybody that was there walked into Ham House garden to see the Rhododendrons—John Bright was there, the greatest speaker in parliament and he is a very famous man (*Later he made the speech at Ellen's wedding—he was Robert Barclay's Uncle by marriage*) he came & spoke to us and Papa introduced me to him. There were also hosts of people there we knew, Buxtons, Fowlers, Barclays, Foxes, and nearly all the friends from the meeting house—The Rhododendrons were very much admired & the people in the garden looked like one large school.

51

Going on the forest.
May 26. 1862.

Geof & Arty picking water violets
with their waterproof legging on—
Johnney in the tree—
Jimmie, Alfred, Lisa, Papa, Mama,
& I walking about—
and 6 ponies.

Geoffrey carrying Emily over the stream.
May 26 1862.

Monday, May 26   This afternoon we had lessons early & then when Papa came home from London we all went a charming ride & drive upon the forest, Mama, Miss Smith & Timmie came in the pony-chair, and Papa, Johnney, Arty, Geof, Alfred & I rode on our ponies. We went to a part of the forest behind "Cookes Folly" a place near Walthamstow, where there was a pond filled with lovely water violets, so when we came to the place we all got off our ponies & tied them each to a separate tree, where they could eat the leaves, & they and the ponychair looked very pretty, then Geof & Arty put on their wading boots, which they had brought with them on purpose to go in the water, & they went in and picked a large bunch of water violets, and pulled some up by the roots, they are a lovely flower, & grow very much in the ponds on the forest about here. Then we went a little walk in the forest & dug up ferns & a few other flowers, & when we came back to the ponychair, we got onto our ponies & rode home—
We have named the new pony "Star of the South", because the great diamond in the Exhibition was called so, so we have named him after it—This morning we found that the chickens had been laying in a place that we did not know of, & there were 18 eggs in it.

Sunday, June 1   Our darling Janet is three years old today, she has been looking forward to it for a long time—
She came down to Prayers for the first time this morning, but did not behave very well, because in the middle she got off her chair & went to Mama.
At dinner time she wore a most *exquisite* wreath of bright blue nemophelas, which suited her very well, for her yellow hair, & red cheeks made the nemophelas look lovely, and she had a nosegay of the same in her hand—
The little children come down to dinner every Sunday—The white kittens are great favourites, they are just beginning to play, we have another lot of kittens born a few days ago.

Wednesday, June 4   This morning at half past twelve Lisa and I went to luncheon at Ham House, they are making grand preparations, because Edward & Emily are coming home this evening, they first went to Egypt up the Nile, they had a very interesting journey in the Holy Land, and met the Prince of Wales several times, then they came home by Constantinople and they are to come home today they were married on the 23 of January this year & have been travelling ever since.   They had made an arch of flowers & evergreens, over the gate at Aman's lodge & had written "Welcome" over it on a piece of calico, then we went back to Ham House & I made a wreath of flowers for each of the little girls & then we anxiously expected their arrival, but we had to wait for a long time, because they had taken out the horses, & men & boys were pulling them up with ropes but at last they did get to the front door, & then we all kissed them & talked & made such a noise that it was difficult to hear ourselves speak.   But at last Aunt Buxton took them up to their room & we all left them to dress for dinner & the carriage came for Lisa, Johnney & I at eight o'clock.

Wednesday, June 25   This morning, Papa, Mama, Emmie, Johnney and I all went to the Exhibition, and had a charming day there, we went principally to the English oil colour painting, which I think are much more beautiful than any of the foreign ones, there are a great many of Gainsborough's and Reynold's there, and a lovely picture of the Prince and Princess of Prussia and their two children, and one of the Queen & the Prince Consort—We also went into the French Court which was most lovely, there were such exquisite peices of spar made up into different things, and Papa bought a lovely little vase made of it, set in gold—

Then there were most beautiful laces, and Babys robes &c they were lovely, and a hood we saw was made entirely of the lace plant. When we had seen heaps of other lovely things that I cannot describe, we had an ice and then went to the International Bazaar.

Last Saturday it was Geofs birthday he was ten years old, he got several presents, and we all had tea in the hay—On Friday poor Papa had a very bad accident at the Brewery, he was in one of the cellars when an immense safe or chest fell onto him & hurt his leg very much, and made a hole in it, he could not walk but they carried him up into his office and sent for Mama directly; it might have been a very bad accident, and he said he never was so near being killed in his life, for the safe was so big and heavy that five men could hardly lift it, but another safe prevented its falling on him & only let it hurt his leg—he slept in the brewery that night & in the morning I went up in the carriage to see him & he most unexpectedly was able to go home in it with Mama, he could not walk or stand but Uncle Charles & Uncle Barclay each held him, & so he managed to get downstairs & into the carriage, some-how I don't know how, the two Uncles had come to see him with Aunt Barclay—he got to Leytonstone very comfortably & then he was helped into the drawingroom, and lay on the sofa the rest of the day.

Tuesday   Papa I am glad to say is getting on very nicely, of course he will not be able to walk for several days, for his leg is stiff & bad, but it does not pain him when he keeps it quite still.

Thursday, Aug 7   Today my Father & Mother took Lisa, Alfred & I to stay till Monday at Foxwarren, where Uncle Charles lives, which is a great treat as Lisa & I have never been there before. We did not start from Leytonstone till the afternoon, & arrived at Foxwarren at 5.

It is a most exquieite house & garden & scenery, I have never seen such an extremely pretty house in my life before, but I cannot the least describe its beauty, all the windows &c are gothic architecture, & there is a great deal of ornament all over & about it.

Friday, Aug 8   Today we went to have luncheon on Newlands corner & when we got there we expected to find some of the Hollands who were to have brought part of the luncheon—they were to have brought bread, & Cake & glasses and Aunt Emily took meat pies, cold chicken, claret & water, so the consequence was, when we got there was no bread to eat, so we had to eat chicken and pies alone & there were no glasses so we drank

out of the bottles, this was great fun. As we drove home we stoped to see Dr. Lushington, who lives at Ockham. He was a great friend of my Grand-father's and helped him in the slave trade. . . .

Friday, Aug 15 J. H.'s birthday   Today our darling John Henry is thirteen years old, he got three nice presents, my Mother gave him a map of London, Lisa & I gave him a beautiful copy of "Lay's of Ancient Rome" & Edith, & Hugh gave hime a "Life of Eliz. Fry". My Father also gave him a cricket bat, but took it away again when he found that he had one—Johnney had a charming new-fashioned cake, iced with chocolate, & patterns of white sugar on the top which was very nice & pretty.

Saturday, August 16   Today it is that lovely Barclay's birthday, he is actually two, already. He was unwell last night, for he had the croop, not very badly I must say, but still it makes me anxious, for whenever any of the brothers, sisters, Father or Mother are *the least* poorly it always makes me dreadfully anxious.
Barclay is *perfectly dilicious* I made him a wreath of small blue & white flowers which suited very well with his yellow hair, & he had a beautiful cake which he & Janet talked about all day, one incessant chatter about

"Barkie's birthday". Effie is the most charming baby I ever saw, she is only 8 months old & she can stand!! if she holds onto something; she wore a ridiculous little pair of shoes for the first time in her life today—she is *trying* to learn to talk, at every thing she sees, but can only manage to say "da".

Janet & Barclay come down to reading every morning, Barclay has much the quietest disposition, so he is very good & is generally quite quiet, but occasionally Janet begins to talk a little & once she began to sing in the middle. She sits on my lap every morning as I play the hymn at reading, & she sings very loud much louder than any one else—& when we say the Lord's Prayer, she puts her little hands together & tries to repeat it after us. . . .

Wednesday, Aug 20   We had a most charming day today, in the first place, 22 of the London Hospital nurses came here to spend the day—My dear Father is so excessively kind to that Hospital,—Six years ago he was elected Chairman, & there ought to be a new Chairman every year, but they found he made such a good one, that they have had him now for six years,—The other day he sent all the nurses to the Exhibition, & gave them each some money to go with. On the whole the nurses seemed to have enjoyed them-selves extremely, they had dinner & tea in the garden, & before they went away I sang to them & then we gave them each a bunch of flowers—22 of the nurses came today & 22 of them will come tomorrow because of course they cannot all come together or they would leave the patients quite alone. On Friday, the day of Uncle Johnston's funeral, it was my dear Father's birthday, he is 41 years old. . . . Andrew Johnstone is still in such deep mourning for his baby, with crepe almost up to the top of his hat. . . . We have got two large glasses of the most delicious honey made by our own bees.

I have got a most beautiful silver knife which Grandmama Gurney gave me in 1853 and at this time of year when there is heaps of fruit I keep it in my delightful underneath pocket where I keep my pocket pencil, thread case, pocket book, plaister, keys, knives, bodkin &c. &c. &c., and all sorts of things that are useful—

The two boys, Arthur & Geoffrey have made a sort of furnace with bricks & mud, & they constantly have bonfires in it;—Alfred is much too clean to get his hands all over mud.

Effie.

Ley Livingstone.   Under the mulberry tree   Alfred   Janet   Murphy

May 1 1864

We have a great many mulberries this year, which are very nice the boys
climb up to the top of the tree, & throw the ripe ones down to us.

Our two Cockatooes "Jacob" and "Esau" are most delightful—Esau makes
a great deal of noise, but talks most rediculously he is quite tame, & the
boys tease him a great deal, he is very handsome & has an orange crest.
Then Jacob is excessively naughty, he is not at all tame, but we want to
take him with us to Northrepps, & he often goes into his cage to feed, but
directly he sees any one coming to shut the door he is out in a moment, so I
do not expect we shall catch him.

Lisa is now considered old enough to wear a bonnet, & she looks much
better in it than she does in a hat, but I do not wish to wear a bonnet yet.

We have now such a remarkable little governess called Miss Sowerby, she
is excessively small, very ugly, wears short petticoats, has five small ringlets
on each side and always looks as though she were silly. She comes twice
a week to teach us flower painting. She seems to have but this one talent &
to know nothing else, for she knows nothing about the Exhibition, & it takes
her three hours to get here.

To Cromer Again

Thursday, Sept 4   Today we spent most of the time in packing up the lesson books and getting everything ready to go to Northrepps tomorrow— (*There follows the description used on p. 31 of "Family Sketchbook a Hundred Years Ago" by E. E. B.*)

Sunday, Sept 7   The beautiful old church at Cromer is being done up, they are putting a new roof, & new windows & repairing it, so the consequence is the Cromerites have made themselves a temporary church in Colne House gardens. This church is a tent, for which Aunt Buxton provided the canvas,

Cromer church
Sept 10 1862.

& the sailors sowed it together, & the sides are made up of the old pews out of the old church. "The Tabernacle" holds about 600 people, & it is always quite full—there is a pulpit in it, taken out of the church, & all the people sit on benches round—so it makes a most delightful church, but what I think is the most rediculous of all, is that the bell of the *real church* rings for the tent.

On Wednesday afternoon we took a most delishous ride on the shore, it was quite low tide & the ponies were very good. They did not mind the sea the least, it was the first time that the Star & Derry had ever been on the shore but they did not mind it the least—

As we were riding home, Alfred was galloping through a rather large, & deep pool (such as often come on the shore)—when that wicked little beast Derry, going at full gallop stopped short in the very middle & sent Alfred over his head, head first & legs up into the water, he went *entirely under* the water & was of course drenched through to the skin but no further harm came—as were were going home the boys got off their ponies at the lodgings, & Papa & I alone, drove those four naughty ponies up to Northrepps, but Franca was most good, & so sensible & wise, he kept a very long way in front of us, & led all the others, & when he got to the gate he waited for us till we should come up & opened it. Each time the boys fall off their ponies, my Father gives them sixpence.

Saturday, Sept 18   We had the most delightful drive, through Salthouse &c. of about 12 miles and when we arrived at Cley Church I never saw anything to equal it I dont think, it was so magnificent, so wonderfully beautiful, inside & out it was perfectly lovely, but I cannot in the least describe it, it is worth going all across England to see, I am so *excessively* fond of antiquities *especially* of old churches and ruins.

On Saturday we had the most delicious walk imaginable—we all met at Northrepps, about 3, and started across the fields towards Cromer, taking naughty Derry with us without saddle or bridle—but his wickedness was the charm of the walk. When we arrived at the bottom of the broad green walk which divided the cottage wood, then we went into the wood & towards Overstrand—But we had to go down two *very* steep places, & Derry galloped down the first, & then the last one was the worst but he went down so cleverly, & it was so steep we really expected to see him come tumbling over to the botton, however he climbed down it to the bottom &

was much applauded by every one who saw him. After that he was the *greatest fun* we kept laughing almost the whole time & he seemed far wiser than any of us. He climbed the hedges that we went over like a cat, & jumped over the furz bushes on the lighthouse hills, & he did not want leading at all, for he always picked out the best path for himself & was just like one of the company.

Oct 1   We had Franca & Derry with sidesaddles, & to Derry we tied the green cart for the babies to ride in—first we went through the cottage woods down to the cottage, but could not get into it or into the flower garden, so we went across the Warren up & down *very* steep hills so steep that our green cart turned over with Chenda & Barclay in it, and Barclay got up laughing & Chenda got up crying, Then Barclay tumbled backwards down a steep bank, headfirst with his legs up in the air, & got up laughing again. After that we found a bakers cart going up to the Hall so Mama who was tired got onto it with some of the little ones & rode on the top of the new bread home.

J.f. 1862.
Mama returning tired in the Bakers' Cart.

61

Sunday, Oct 5   Well now I must tell you that there has for some days past been a wreck on the shore—it mistook the light of the lighthouse for a fishing boat (which was very silly) and so they ran strait ashore, & it was a good deal broken—all the men escaped, but the Cromer fisherman thought it was *their duty* to use the life boat, so instead of bringing the men *from* the wreck, they took the men *to* the wreck, this was a most odd idea—so the wreck lay for about a week on the shore, & today they got a tug from Yarmouth & took it to be mended.   It was most naughty to take the wreck away on Sunday, though if they had left it it would have been a great trial of faith for the poor man if he had left it there, for the next high tide it *might* have been dashed to pieces—so what with Cousin Edward and the wreck the congregation of the tabernacle was very much thinned—because lots of people went to hear Cousin Edward preach at Sidestrand, and enormous quantities of people were on the jetty and shore watching the wreck going away—But the consequence was as the congregation of the pretty little Sidestrand Church, after a most beautiful sermon from Cousin Edward, were coming out of Church, we saw the *wreck* going away, towed by the steam tug from Yarmouth—it was a most lovely view, & it was very interesting to see the helpless old wreck towed off by the tug.

On Tuesday we had a delightful walk in the cottage woods, but unfortunately we had no one to take care of us, so of course there was a war going on amongst the boys the whole time.

On Sunday morning it rained very hard so we had two carriages to take us to church we were such a large party—and in the afternoon we all went to church at Cromer because it is the first time they have had church in the real church since it has been repaired, so now they have deserted the Tabernacle and have gone again to the old church—the church of course is not nearly done but the roof is on, and the windows are not put in neither are the pretty new pews—but they have removed the seats from the Tabernacle into the church.

The Lord Bishop of London is staying at Cromer so on Tuesday evening he came and dined at Northrepps Hall, he and Mrs. Tate, we all admire him so very much—he once lost five children altogether in six weeks, when he was Dean of Carlisle.   When he came to dine here he gave us a charming Bible reading after dinner & explained Gal. III.

I never saw such a lovely baby as Effie is, she tries to talk but cant exactly manage it, so she makes all sorts of noises, so pretty, & she hardly ever cries, she can creep anywhere. Papa says "No one else has such a nice baby".

Sunday, Oct 26   The Tabernacle is demolished & the church is fit for use again—The church looks *charming* it has three beautiful architectural windows, & Francis' new clock looks very nice; but of course all the new pews are not put into the church so they have got benches to sit upon till the pews are put up. Really the church inside looks lovely, but the worse of it is the old galeries are still there which spoils it very much, but Mr. Fitch is afraid that if they are taken down there will not be room for all the fishermen & the poor people.

Nov 4   On Friday we were busy all day making up a large bonfire to burn tomorrow it was great fun, for my Father staid at home all the after-noon, the gardiners came to help and all the boys, and all the babes, so we were a fine party and we spent such a nice afternoon, & got up quite a large heap of wood, dried asparagrass, old beanstorks, &c.

'PICKING UP WOOD IN THE DRY POND'

Saturday, 15th Nov   The parrots are most delightful; Northrepps would not be half what it is now without these charming birds.

There are two very large, *snowy white* cockatoos who fly about making a great noise, and looking very handsome—Then there are two small, but pure white cockatoos, with bright scarlet eyes, These two come to the nursery every morning when the children are at breakfast and knock at the window till they get some bread and butter, and then they eat all the butter and throw away all the bread, and they go to a great many other windows where they know they can get anything to eat.   Then there is an extremely handsome green parrot with a golden patch on the top of his head; and he is the most delightful to the children I think because he talks so much, and says so many funny things he can sing "Oh dear what can the matter be", and says all sorts of other things—Then there are quantities of other green parrots with scarlet tails; altogether there 24—counting cockatoos and all.

Some of the parrots are excessively fond of Future (the gardiner) They sit upon his shoulder, and kiss him, and stand upon his large basket which he

always carries with him.

The mice at Northrepps Hall are most amusing, I do not think that there is a single room in the house that you cannot hear the mice in the walls, generally at night, but very often in the day—

There is one particular room at the top of the stairs which swarms with mice & immense rats—this room goes by the name of "The mice room"— Then the night nursery is crammed with mice the maids are really afraid to sit there in the evening, because the mice are so *impudent* that they come out onto the floor and sit upright with their ears pricked up and look at the maids, then they have races all about the rooms (in the walls) and make the most *furious* noise, far, far more than anyone could have expected, I have seen rats, almost as large as leverets, running about in the garden—and even in middle of the day the rats come out & *look at* the children as they are dressing.

When the Charles Buxton's were all here there were 40 people sleeping *in* the house! and *everyday* Maria (the cook) gets from Breese (the celebrated Cromer baker) *18* large loaves of bread, and on Saturday she brings in more than thirty! !

Sunday, Nov 16   Our last Sunday at Northrepps.
In the afternoon 12 of us walked to church, and were *all* late, I do not think we ever were late before for Northrepps church.
On Sunday evening we had our last nice apocraphal reading—every Sunday evening Grandmother invites us all to late dinner with her, and today we had three beautiful pheasants in one dish—After dinner we all get ourselves a *large* and *old* Bible. It is the fashion of the day to read out of large Bibles, and I do not think that hardly any house in England has so many in which is the apocrapher, For the last few Sundays we have been reading Judith, and today we finished it. . . .

1863

Jan 24, 1863   During the last month this house has been more like a hospital than anything else, for children, servants and all have had extremely bad colds, Effie was the worst, her cold went onto her chest, and she coughed and wheezed so very much, that Papa and Mama sent for Dr. Peacock, everyday from London because she was so ill. Then poor Barclay and Janet have also been ill, with very bad coughs which we thought was whooping cough but they are also better now, tho' in getting better they are *excessivly* cross.

On the 17th January it was my birthday, I was fifteen years old. Now that our precious little Effie is recovering from her illness, she sleeps in another room with Eleanor, just to get a little change of air—so the consequence is, I have to go and sleep in the night nursery and take care of Emily, Janet and Barclay, this I enjoy very much.

Sunday, Feb 7   Today we were nine at Sunday dinner which we have not been for a long time, of course we could not be 10, because of John Henry being at School—I always sit between Barclay & Effie, and take care of them and cut up their meat, but no one who does not see them now *can imagine* how sweet they are. Effie was a year old last December, so now of course she comes down to dinner with the others on Sunday. My mother makes her babies feed themselves, almost as soon as they can hold a spoon, but Effie always eats her by picking it up in her fingers like a little bird.

Thursday, Feb 26   Today Mama and Louisa went up to London to see some schools, because as Louisa is going to school at Easter it is necessary to decide which she shall got to at once. She is delighted to go, but how *I* would hate it!

Janet and Barclay are the most precious little pair I ever saw, no one's else's children can be compared to them, Janet is three years old, & Barclay is two. They are both very fond of me, & I almost always take them walks in the garden, & they are with me all day except when I am at lessons, they come to Reading every morning, & I am sorry to say sometimes do not behave very well, sometimes Janet sings most tremendously loud, far louder than anybody else in the room, so it causes quite a sensation, & when we stop in between the verses she goes on just as though there were no verses. Barclay does not sing so loud, but he fidgits more, sometimes he is quite naughty, a few days ago in the middle of the hymn he was fidgiting so much that suddenly he fell down flat on the floor, & we could hardly help laughing, he always sits by me, so I have to try and keep him in order. He rolls his hoop so very nicely, he never will use a wooden one, but can roll an iron one just as well & better than many much older boys than he, though he is only a baby; and he has quite an art of spinning a top, rubbing it between his dear plump fat hands to make it spin. But with all his good qualities he is a great coward. The other day we went to Ham House to see the lambs & kids, some of them were quite tame, & ran after us like little dogs, but he was so very much affraid of them that we had to hunt them away, & if any came near he began to cry.

Effie is also a most charming child, though I do no think she will grow up so pretty as either of the other two, she is extremely fond of a good romp, & laughs more than any of them, she always comes down to see us while we are at breakfast, & eats Jam & cream.

Friday, March 6   Prissy & Isabelle Johnston came last night, to stay with us for a little while. They come up principally to go and see the entry of the Princess Alexandria of Denmark who is to come to London tomorrow from a yacht at Gravesend & is to be married to the Prince of Wales on Tuesday the 10th.

Prissy & Isabelle helped us to make large favors of white calico for the horses.

The Royal Wedding

Saturday   We have just had a grand day in seeing the Princess Alexandria. As we drove up to London, many houses were adorned with flags, and places for aluminations on Tuesday, which is the Prince's wedding day, and as we got nearer London,there were thousands & thousands of people all walking towards King William Str, to see the sight, so we drove up to Uncle Edmund's office in Lombard Str, & there were lots of people assembled, then each gentleman took a lady, to the house in King William Str where we were to be, but unfortunately they had to leave Johnney, Arty, Geof, Alfred Emily and I, in 65 Lombard Str as there were not enough gentlemen to take us, so we waited a long time, & at last Papa reappeared saying that he could only take one at a time as there was the most fearful crush of people, so he took Johnney, & then very soon after *happily*, one of Aunt Buxton's servants came & took Geoffrey, then Papa came back again after infinite dificulty & took Arthur, & carried Emily at the same time under his arm, then happily Buscal, & another kind man came, & said he would take Arthur & I, . . . it was the most wonderful crush I ever saw . . . however we did at last get there, & Mama said I looked quite white as I always do when I am frightened . . .when we looked out of the window that broad Str looked like one sea of heads . . . we saw carriages of grand people going to meet the Princess at the Bricklayer's arms station who were to follow in the procession, & then about 2-45, the procession began to pass . . . at last came the 6 Royal carriages. In the first three there were different Danish ladies & gentlemen, in the fourth came Alexandra's lovely little sister "Thyra", who was about 10 years old, & was so pretty, she sat with her face to the horses & bowed at all the people on each side, in the same carriage were two other ladies & her baby brother. In the fifth carriage came the princess "Dagmar", another of Alexandra's sisters, she was grown up, & was very pretty, & very like Alexandra, so she did not bow to disguish her from our princess; she was dressed in white, & at first everybody thought it was her herself but then at last she came, really, & all raised a loud shout when she came, & she bowed so nicely, on each side & we thought her so pretty, by her side sat her mother the Princess Louise, & oposite her sat the Prince of Wales, & her father the Prince Christian, brother to the king of Denmark. As she came every body began to cheer, & to wave their pocket handkerchiefs, & she stopped for a minute exactly opposite our window, after her came a quantity of life guards on beautiful black horses, & when she had gone bye all the mob began to rush and tear after her, making the most furious crush. Then we all came down & walked back to Lombard Str where we found out two carriages, & packed into them & began to drive home. . . .

Tuesday March 10, 1863   To-day is the day of the Prince and Princess's wedding. Of course we shall hear nothing of it till to-morrow. . . . At 6 o'clock a large van came round to take us to see the illuminations and we all got into it with the Pattesons so there were 17 of us . . . there were some very pretty stars and Prince of Wales feathers all made by hollow tubes, with little jets in them out of which the gas came, so that when it was set on fire it looked very pretty indeed, there were also a great many A. A.s meaning "Albert" and "Alexandra" and P W for Prince of Wales, all illuminated with gas. . . . Then we saw the Royal Exchange, it had a row of gas along the roof & the text "The earth is the Lord's" etc. was made of light & the pillars of it were encircled with little lamps all round them. . . .

Wednesday, March 11, 1863   This morning we employed all our time in reading about the wedding. . . .

Saturday, March 14   To-day Aunt Barclay, Edith, Hugh, Ada, Alice, Papa, Lisa, Edward & Emily and myself all went by train to see the chapel and state rooms at Windsor, which are now open so that anybody may go and see them without tickets, and special trains to Windsor were running every half hour. Just before we got to the Windsor station we quite stopped as there was a train just in front of us, and then Aunt Barclay found out that she had left all her tickets behind with Mr. Frederick Barclay, so she screamed out of the window to Martin who was several carriages off and gave him full directions as to what he was to say when she sent the guard to him to explain about the tickets so that the whole train heard what she was saying. When we got to the castle there were a great number of people, and we were let in by hundreds into the chapel. We had first to go through a large sort of house, erected just for the wedding, which consisted of a sort of large hall in the middle, and smaller rooms all round it, for the different people, there was one for the Bride, one for the Bridegroom, & so on for lots of other people, and they were all most beautifully decorated. We went through the chapel and saw the places where Aunt and Uncle Bunsen, and Fowell and Lady Victoria had sat. In the chapel there were no decorations except for scarlet carpets and footstools. Then we walked about in the castle gardens a little and went and saw the stables and then came home.

Monday, March 16, 1863   To-day we drove to see Aunt and Uncles Charles. While we were there Sir Henry Holland came in who is Aunt Emily's father, and one of the grandest doctors in the kingdom, and he said that he had been to the Prince's wedding and told us a story about the little Prince of Prussia, who had appeared at the wedding in a Scotch dress, which all the nation wondered at, and he said the reason of it was, that he had brought over from Prussia a little regimental "coatee" to wear at the wedding, but when we came to Windsor Prince Arthur and Leopold were so much amused with it, that they cut off the tails of it, and so of course he could not wear it, and his mother had to find him up an old coat of Leopold's to wear, which happened to be a Scotch dress. Then Sir Henry Holland told us about the Archbishop of Canterbury, who, after the wedding had tried to walk back again to Windsor station to go home, but suddenly came into such a dense crowd that he was quite frightened and called out to a policeman who was standing near "I'm the Archbishop of Canterbury, how shall I be *saved?*" So the policeman said "I cannot get near you, but go your Grace and cling on behind that carriage, so will you get along." So he got behind the carriage and there he found also clinging behind the carriage Thackery the novelist and Lady Cranworth. When Lady Cranworth saw the Archbishop she said "Before your Grace came, I was ashamed of my position but now that you are come I am proud of it". It was odd that 3 such different people should meet in such a place.

1863

March 27, Friday   To-day we all went to see the British Museum. Aunt Bunsen knows Professor Owen, a man who gives his whole life to studying antiquities particularly fossils and skeletons, & so she asked him to let us all go with him to see some of the things there, & he said he would explain it. We went to see the great bones and he explained a great many of them, but he spoke in such a low voice that some could not hear, the principal thing that we had come to see was a most remarkable fossil bird which had been found imbedded in stone, & only discovered last year, but it lived such a long time ago, that when it was alive none of the chalk was made, and as all the chalk is made of old animals ground to powder who lived long before the Deluge, it must have lived millions of years ago. But it was most remarkably perfect and we could see each feather and each bone, but the head was gone, probably it had been eaten by some wild beast. . . . Louisa is going to school on Easter Tuesday at Miss Clarence's near Brighton where there are 27 girls.

Good Friday, April 3   This morning we went to church & in the afternoon, we took a walk as usual, taking Derry in his carriage for the little ones to ride in; Henry, Edmund, Louis and Francis also came with us, we went onto the forest, and stopped by a high bank of gravel which had been thrown up from the gravel pits, & all the boys went and played in the gravel pits some of which were very deep & full of water, they set Ford's perambulator afloat sometimes, & were up to all kinds of mischief. We all sat on the top of the hill, and once as Aunt Barclay was seating herself on it she came down with such a bump that she shook the whole hill, which was really a very large one.

Visit to the North

On Saturday, April 11, Papa, Mama, John Henry, Alfred, Emily, and I went to Carlisle to spend about a week with Aunt and Uncle Head. We had a comfortable journey going all across England in 8 hours, and having the luxury of the beautiful family carriage. We had plenty to do, work, books etc, & when we got to Preston we had a little dinner, & in the station we saw an old lady who filled & lighted her pipe and then smoked in the train. We reached Carlisle at 6.10, but the last hour of our journey had been so enlivened by the exquisite scenery, of mountains, rivers, valley etc. that we did not feel fatigued.

We have had 2 nice letters from Louisa at her school, she says she likes Miss Clarence very much, & is very happy there.

Tuesday, April 14 We went a drive with Aunt Sarah to see the working classes of poor women who have nothing to do because of the cotton famines all about Carlisle and Lancashire. I do not think I have mentioned the Cotton Famine before but during the last winter the people of Lancashire & Cumberland have been in fearful distress and would have been starving if it were not for the relief fund which comes in to the managers from all parts of England—it is all caused by the dreadful civil war in America, the Northern against the Southern States, and so if the people are fighting they cannot plant cotton, and so all the mills are stopped and so all the poor people are thrown out of work.

. . . My father and the boys went to fish but caught nothing.

Wednesday, April 15 Today we have had the most delicious excursion, to see Naworth Castle, Lanacost Abbey the Roman Wall and Gilsland. . . .

Saturday, April 18 Today we went a delightful excursion to Scotland to see Melrose Abbey, Abbotsford, where Sir Walter Scott lived, and Dryborough Abbey. I had never been in Scotland before and it was the most lovely scenery all the way to Melrose and we read several pieces of poetry out of Scott's life about the places to which we were going. . . From Melrose we took a fly to Abbotsford where Sir Walter Scott used to live, it is about 3 miles from Melrose and a very handsome, rather modern house; noone live there, and there is no real heir, but a little heiress 11 years old, who comes in the summer. Inside were all the things remaining just as they were when Sir Walter died, and there are a great many busts & pictures of him. All the rooms are most beautifully furnished, and the ceilings copied from Melrose and the other Abbeys, all carved in oak wood. The hall was all hung with old armour swords &c. The outside of the house is very hand-some, and close by is the river Tweed. . . . Then we drove back again to Melrose, ate some mutton chops, and bought one or two large photographs of the Abbey and then set off again to see Dryborough Abbey. . . .

Monday, April 20   In the afternoon we all drove into Carlisle and saw the biscuit manufactures, & then Papa bought a box of them to take to the Leathams, they were delicious, & we ate some directly they came out of the oven.

Tuesday, April 21   Today we moved from Rickerby to Hemsworth. We had a tiresome journey, & changed 5 times, so that in the time we took going from Carlisle to Leeds, we might have gone from Carlisle to London, it was rather a teadeous journey, and was pouring with rain most of the way. . . .

Wednesday, April 22   This morning Gurney Leatham asked us all to be photographed, for he takes phottgraphs on glass, of every body that goes there he takes them very well indeed and has done a great many.

Sunday, April 25 (*Back home*)   A most delicious-day, really too hot, we put on all our thinest Summer things; in our walk home from church we found a lark's nest in the meadow, with three eggs in, it is very early still for lark's nests.

The meadow is now put up for hay, so all the cows sheep and ponies are in the field near the house, and they look so very pretty. No one has such nice ponies as we have, or cows really the cows are such wonderfully beautiful creatures, there are six of them and all Alderney's, besides five very pretty

Bucky   Janet Emily and Arthur.
going to water the gardens.

heifers, & often there are calves which we generally eat, and they are really most delicious—Our milk is like *other people's* cream, it is so beautiful, and delicious, we use it as clotted cream sometimes because it is so thick, and it is almost solid. There are now two litters of young rabbits, so very pretty, we have three old ones, but the mothers do not the least care for their children, so we have to feed them on milk and bran. I wonder they live.

Monday, May 4   On Monday morning Louisa went back to her school, she is supremely happy and so enjoys being with the girls, with whom she "romps" as she says, and they like her very much, the name they call her is "Bucky", a nickname for Buxton. Last Saturday one of our lovely Alderney cows died, she had a calf and then died, she was one of the prettiest, and the darkest of them all.

There is a most exquisite little chaffinches nest close by the path near the green house, and as we go to the five's court we have to pass quite close to her but she does not the least care. The fives court was built about a month ago between the Chickenyard and Hothouse, Papa and the boys play at it whenever they can.

Thursday, May 7   This morning I went up with Mama, Papa, Hilda and

Edith in the carriage to one of the May meetings at Exeter Hall, it was the city mission society and very interesting it was, a Mr Bevan was in the chair, and Lord Shaftesbury made a very nice speech and so did several other gentlemen whose names I do not know, but it was very interesting, and we girls took out our works, which was very pleasant. Then we went to Mr Toynbee, Mama's ear doctor, because she has been rather deaf lately.

Saturday, May 9   This afternoon we went riding and driving 38, onto the forest, we thought we were a nice family party. But the great take off to the whole thing was the immense crowds of horrid, disgusting, detestable little green caterpillars, about ½ of an inch long, which hung in profusion o the trees, such innumerable quantities of them and so nasty, directly we came near a tree they used to get upon & hundreds of them stuck to us, so that we had to brush them off. But the forest besides that was beautiful and we were such a nice party that we quite enjoyed it, & ate up a whole large tin of biscuits which Aunt Barclay had brought, a large cake, & quantities of milk & gingerbeer.

'BISHOP OF RIPON SPEAKING AT THE CITY MISSION EXETER HALL, MAY, 1865 (*left*), AND BISHOP OF CARLISLE; CHURCH MISSIONARY MEETING, MAY 1, 1866 (*right*)

Friday, May 15   This evening Aunt Sarah (*Head*) Aunt Buxton, Aunt Bunsen, Aunt Leatham, & Aunt Barclay are all dinning here, it is so pleasant to have the 5 Aunts & sisters all together, they all stood in a row in the evening, & we decided that Aunt Leatham was the tallest, Mama the prettiest and Aunt Barclay the naughtiest, the six sisters have not been all together since Aunt Sarah's wedding on May 1st 1858.

Effie still continues to eat her meat with her fingers, she will not have a spoon and she almost lives on cold mutton. I am sure no children in the world are so nice as Janet, Barclay and Effie. Janet is a perfect little lady, quite small for her age, but so excessively pretty, she has bright yellow hair, a pure white forehead, bright red cheeks, & bright blue eyes. She and Barclay are extremely affecate to each other, sometimes they put their arms round each other's necks and kiss, but very often they are not quite so sweet. By all strangers they are taken for twins because they are so exactly the same size, though there is 14 months between them, Janet will be 4 on the first of June, & Barclay will be 3 in August.

I have got now a lovely swallowtail butterfly I had two but one died a few days ago, they live about 10 days, I have crisallises which Papa buys in London, & they are extremely nice to keep, for they are no trouble because they are hatched *quite tame*. I always make this one live all day on the nosegay in the middle of the drawingroom table, and he never attempts to fly away, & in the evening he gets under a leaf, shuts up his wings & goes to sleep.

Tuesday, June 4   Last night there was a tremendously grand ball in Guildhall, and 2000 people went, the Prince and Princess of Wales & all sorts of nobility, gentry, &c. and Aunt Barclay went, with Uncle Gurney (*both Quakers*) she was dressed in a lovely dun-coloured silk, & most exquisite natural wreath of orkids, worth £20 a sprig, & the dress made in the most lovely way open in front of the skirt and showing white muslin. Aunt Barclay says it was a grand sight, she saw the Princess well, & says that she was dressed in a white dress with a coronet of pearls, the Prince looked excessively silly and plain, as people say he always does.

Thursday, June 11   Today Papa took us all down by the afternoon train to Longparish to be there till Saturday.

Friday, June 12   We were wonderfully comfortable in our little room at the little "Plough Inn" last night, the three boys who slept in two beds in the next room to us, being only divided by old shutters woke us up early, so Hilda and I as we could not sleep, began to knitt in bed, as we had been expressly told not to get up early.   Then we breakfasted at 8, & about 9 started a walk first to see some of the most lovely little Hampshire cottages all over-grown with roses and creepers, & the old church with its beautiful churchyard.   The river is called the Test, & abounds with Trout, it is excessively pretty, & we went rambling all over a bay in search of grasses, and flowers, where of course we got wet up to our knees.   At one they brought us out some luncheon in the carriers cart, very good it was, and Aunt Bunsen also came from the inn, & then Hilda & I went a further walk by the sides of the river and found quantities of maiden-hair, or as some people call it quaking grass. . . .

'DRAWING NEAR THE RIVER AT LONGPARISH'

Monday, June 15   Aunt Bunsen since she has been here has made quite a change in the garden, all the pailings in the field on the front of the house are taken away so as to make a sort of open lawn, of course it is an improvement to the garden, but the worst of it is that the ponies have to be sent away and the cows only tethered.

Saturday, June 20   All today we have been entensely busy preparing for a party of 2500 volonteers from London, who came down commanded by Uncle Charles onto the flats and there they fought a sham fight.

Early in the morning arrived a cart from "Boote's" containing 20 cheeses such enormouse things, larger than I could carry, each weighing lbs 28, and were sold at 8 pence a lb. so that each cheese cost nearly £1. Then there came 600 large loaves of bread, steaming hot from the oven, & as we were all cutting them up they burnt out fingers so much that they quite hurt us. Then there were 6 large tables put out in the field, & on these were put all this immense quantity of bread, & cheese cut up into small pieces, also a large tub of iced water and plenty of beer.

The volunteers at last came in several special trains, & our horses were very much frightened as they passed us, but they went directly onto the flats and there wasted an hour or two as all soldiers do, till they began the fight, which consisted in fighting for and taking the old house of Mr Wigram's which stands on the flats. The brewery corps were inside the house and they were driven from it by the others, then after having some more fighting in the avenues they all marched into our field where they ate & drank as much as they would & then went to the station. Afterwards we found that they had left a good deal of bread & cheese, which was given away to the poor people, & amongst other things three and a half of those immense cheeses were stolen, evidently by someone who had got in amongst the volonteers & carried them off. They were not all gone till 9.45, & they cheered Mama at her window as they went away, because she was not well enough to walk downstairs.

Sunday, June 21   Today is Geoff's birthday he is 11 years old. He got several presents and we all had tea in the hay.

Saturday, June 27   Today 16 of us went to the Christal Palace to see a splendid show of roses. We drove to Blackwall, there took a steam boat to

"Let I drop it" Baby says —

Greenwich, & from there drove in three flys to the Palace which was about 6 miles. There was a great crowd of people, but some of the roses were most lovely, & it was a splendid sight to see, we took the names of as great many. Then after eating an ice and walking through several of the courts and garden, we came back the same way as we went and got to Leytonstone soon after 8. But as we drove home from blackwall, Korah, the best of the three carriage horses fell down and broke his knees. He was called Korah because when Papa first bought him, he was living at Ham House, and one day when Barnet was leading them out of the stable to be put into the carriage the ground gave way, & one of them fell right down into a large deep hole, which once had been a deep sistern but had been covered over with such bad wood that it broke, the horse was got out after some time with considerable difficulty, he poor thing making desperate plunges all the time to try & get his feet out of the quantity of mud which was at the bottom, but at last they succeeded in putting the kitchen tablecloth under his body & so when the horse made an effort & the people too, they drew him out all covered with foam & extremely exhausted and so his name was called Korah in rememberance of being swallowed up.

July 1st   At the sale for the new church at Stratford was the *whole* family, Gurney's, Pellys, Frys, Buxtons, & Sheppards, I could not write them all down if I were to try.

Wednesday, July 15   This evening was the great dinner that is annually given to all the clerks at Blackwall, and as Papa, Uncle Charles & Towell were driving there they went into a celebrated shop there where are sold all kinds of beasts and birds, Bears, Lions, Tigers, Elephants, Crocodiles, Cockatoos and anything imaginable that you like to order he will get for you. So they went in & saw all these beasts, bought some parrots for Northrepps and some for Fox Warren, and besides that Uncle Charles actually bought a crocodile! There were two, one about 7 feet long, in a long narrow box and the other about 2 feet long, Uncle Charles bought the latter, and it is to live at Fox Warren on Raw meat.

Thursday, July 16, 1863   Today was a grand day at Cheam school. Once every year Mr Tabor invites the fathers and mothers of all the boys to come down and see the prizes given away. It is called "Speech day," because a great many of the boys learn long pieces of poetry, Latin, Greek, plays and famous pieces of writing to say before all the company. This year Mama & Papa were invited but as Mama was not strong enough to go she let Louisa and I go instead of her with Papa. So Louisa and I went up by the half past twelve train from Leytonstone had luncheon at the Brewery and then went by train from London Bridge to Cheam, getting there about 3.30 and found John Henry waiting for us at the station. A great many of the parents of the other boys also came by that train and were arriving all the afternoon, John Henry was delighted to see us, and about 4 o'clock we all went into the boys schoolroom where the speeches were going to be, the boys who did not speak were not allowed to come in, but it was quite filled up with ladies and gentlemen. The Speeches were most splendidly delivered I never heard such good speaking, it began by one saying Macauley's "*Ivry*". Then there came a long latin speech and several others, amongst which I thought "Lord Chatham's last speech" was the best and the play of Shakespeare about Hubert and Prince Arthur. Then at the end there was Moliere's play of "La Mariage forcee," which was done most capitally, and at the end before we all went away we saw the prizes given away, each boy was called in by Mr Tabor, & then it was given to him, John Henry got the two prizes for Mathematics and French in the IIIrd class, such beautiful books they were, two vols of a beautifully illustrated Milton, then we all went out and stayed in the garden till teatime at half past six. All the gentlemen & ladies went indoors to a splendid dinner and all the 93 boys had tea on the lawn, and the girls that had come to see is also had tea on the lawn but at a different table, after tea we had to wait till about 9 o'clock for the fireworks, first two very large balloons went up with fireworks, & all the others were most beautiful they cost £200 so they ought to have been good. . . .

Friday, July 24   This morning Mr. and Mrs. Schon from Chatham came with all their children and four black people, they come once every year to spend a day here, and do enjoy themselves so intensely, this is the sixth year they have come. This time they only brought four negroes but generally they bring 6 or 7, but Derogoo came, and the other three were black ladies, besides all Mr & Mrs Schon's party amounting on the whole to 15 persons. They came from London Bridge Station in a large omnibus, and were here to luncheon and then some of them went out driving with Mama, some play croquet some went walks all the boys and Derrogou played at cricket.

Saturday, July 25   My Grandmother is poorly and so Papa and Louisa went down to Northrepps to see her today but they only stay till Monday, Mama took them in the carriage to the Shoreditch Station, and then Barnett thinking that she was gone with them came away and left her in London so she had to come down in the train but having not a penny in her pocket she first had to go to the Brewery and borrow 5/- of the butler there, and then she came back to the station and walked up to our house in the pouring rain.

Journey to France

Friday, July 31   We are very busy today as tomorrow Mama, Papa, Louisa, John Henry and myself are going to start for France, to spend a week in Paris.

On *Sunday* hardly any one in Dover went to church, hosts of steamers and trains arrived and it was just as noisy as a weekday.—I wore my new cloke that Grandmama gave me and *it was so* much admired, it is such a beauty of Grenadine.

Monday   On arriving at Calais it was curious to me to see for the first time a foreign town and hear all the people jabber French, but we had a wretched railway journey to Paris it was so intensely and intolerably hot and dusty, and besides that there was a wretched woman who would shut all the windows, so we were glad enough to get to Paris. We waited for a few minutes to have our luggage searched and then got into a sort of omnibus with a large gray Flemish horse with bells round his neck, all the horses here have them. Our rooms are very nice overlooking the Tuileries and the large Rue de Rivoli which is most entertaining with all the horses and carriages.

Inner Castle.
Aug. 3. 1863.

Tuesday, August 4   After breakfast we staid in till about 11 to write letters and then started to fly first to see the further end of the Rue Rivoli then through the court yard of the palace of the Tuillaries, and of the Louvre, called the Place de la Carousal, where also the beautiful arch built by Napoleon stands . . . and then on to the Bois de Boulogne, it is a large wood very pretty, and about nine o'clock there were hosts of carriages each with 2 lamps on, and the sight was most beautiful to see them all, the whole road at a distance glittered with them and as we were driving home we suddenly saw that the Empress had passed us, so we immediately turned back and at last got a sight of her, but it was so dark we could not see her very well, she was dressed in white in a carriage with four horses and one other lady with her.

Wednesday, Aug 5   This morning Papa Mama, Louisa, John Henry and I went to see the pictures in the Louvre, they were most beautiful we saw some very celebrated ones, especially the one of Murillo's "Virgin" being carried up to heaven by the cherubim, a great many people were copying the pictures. At 2 o'clock we went with an order to see the Tuilleries but I do not think it was very nice. . . .

F

Saturday, August 8   Mama was quite unwell all the morning but at 1 o'clock she was well enough to go on to Amiens by the next train.

Monday, Aug 10 Amiens   This morning early Mama was excessively poorly, almost too faint to speak, but as the day went on she got better, and though we have given up all though of going away today I should not be vastly surprised if we leave here for Calais tomorrow.
This morning we took a drive to see St Acheul an interesting place as lately the workmen have pretended to find in the gravel old weapons of flint in the gravel, so trying to make out that men lived before Adam and therefore the Bible was not true, great interest was taken in the place about 2 months ago, but now it is discovered to be merely a pretence and that the workmen as they dug the gravel out of the pit had put them in and pretended to find them. They were mearly pieces of flint chipped and one side to made a sort of edge, but I did not see that they were very different to other flints. Then we drove to see the Hotel de Ville, the place where Napoleon signed the treaty of Amiens in 1803. Towards the end of the afternoon my Mother feeling much better said that she felt well enough to start tonight. We had a nice journey in the night to Calais, arriving there at 2 o'clock on Tuesday morning, we directly went to the hotel where we staid for the remainder of the night. The next morning Papa has a very bad headache, so we had to stay at the hotel till we crossed in the afternoon, and when we got to Dover we got into the train and went home, we took a carriage from the London station to Leytonstone, they were intensely surprised to see us.

Monday, Aug 17, 1863   Last night Mr Adams' house was burnt down, he is a gentleman who lives close here, in a single house, and it was burnt, in the middle of the night Mama saw it and sent some of the servants to see what had happened, happily no one was hurt, Papa invited Mr Adams to come in here with his family but they had gone somewhere else. The fire broke out about 11, immediately on finding it out they sent all the children, Mrs. Adams and the maids to a house near, the engines from Woodford, Stratford, and London were sent for but unfortunately when they got there the pipes were too short and they had to wait an hour longer for some more. All this time the house was burning furiously out of the windows the flames burst forth, and as it was a very windy night all the smoke was blown away and it looked grand. They succeeded in saving all the horses carriages and a great many thing out of the house, such as the furniture pictures &c. But the worst of it was that such hosts of things were stolen hosts and hosts of people, (Mr Adams thought about 2000) came to see it and most of the men broke into the burning house and stole, *more than half* the things, all their clothes, Mrs Adam's beautiful silk dresses and all were stolen, this was far worse than if they had been burnt.

Saturday, August 29

> "The large and beautiful iron ship Baroda is the first vessel launched from the yard of the Millwall Iron Works and Ship-building Company, who have in hand the Northumberland frigate and other extensive commissions for the Government. The Baroda, a vessel of 2,091 tons and 400-horse power, is one of those two we have mentioned as being intended for the Peninsular and Oriental Company's service."

Today we have all been to Millwall to see the lauch of the "Baroda". When we arrived at Millwall we went first to see the largest piece of iron in the world wrought. When it came out of the huge furnace we could not go near it was tremendously hot and so brilliant I could scarcely look at it. It was a very dangerous place to be in I think for there were large pieces of red hot iron lying all about, and great sparks flew from the furnaces in all directions. About 1.30, the owner of the ship and iron works took us all to the ship, he asked Aunt Buxton to christen her, she would not, but said that Emmie would. They were very much pleased to have her do it and we all had to get up into a sort of raised platform under the bow of the ship higher than all the other people, which was meant for the ladies and gentlemen. About 2 o'clock when everything was ready the master gave the word of command, she threw the bottle at the ship, it broke, and the instant after the ship went away at a great pace, it was grand to see it go, so quickly but perfectly upright, then directly she got into the water she heaved right over onto her side. Everybody was really frightened, they thought she had gone right over so that the whole crowd ceased cheering, but then again she righted herself, and turned up the river, but so much did go over that three men were thrown into the water. She looked beautiful in the river and they directly began to tow her back again opposite the yard to put in her engines &c.

Northrepps 1863

Friday, Sept 4   For the last few days we have been very busy getting ready and packing up for going to Northrepps and today was fixed upon for going there. Papa, Mama, Johnney, Arty, Geof, Alfred, Emily, Janet, Barclay, Doctor Pagenstecker, Effie and myself went in the same train besides three maids, three men servants eight horses, one dog and a carriage. My Father had engaged the beautiful family carriage to take us all down. Doctor Pagenstecker goes down with us to take care of Arthur, Geoffrey, and Alfred at the lodgings, because Miss Smith is gone for her holiday. Mama has engaged No. 6 on the Terrace at Cromer for the boys.

The four boys and Doctor went in the second class compartment and I took care of the three babies in the first class, which was like a little drawing-room with Papa and Mama, they were very good, and I put them to lie down in the "night nursery," and at 1, had our dinner. On arriving at Norwich we got all the ponies and horses out of the train, and Papa, Johnney, Arthur, Geoffrey and myself rode all the way to Northrepps.

Tuesday, Sept 15   Today my dear grandmother is 80 years old she was born in the year 1783, and was one of 12 children (*the celebrated Gurneys of Earlham*) and now she and Uncle Dan are the only two left. Uncle Dan was the youngest of all. Grandmama's mother died when Aunt Catherine her eldest sister was 17 years old, and she was quite a mother to all her brothers and sisters. My grandmother has had 11 children only 2 of which are now living; my Father and Uncle Charles. Her little girl Susanna died in the year 1811, she was remarkable for her exquisite beauty. In 1820 she lost 4 children in about 6 weeks, from whooping cough and measles, they are all buried in Hendon church yard, their names were Thomas Fowell, Hannah, Rachel Gurney, and Louisa. About 1838 her son John Henry died he was 16 years old, Aunt Johnston died in 1852 and in 1858 Uncle Buxton and Aunt Chenda Hamond died within three days of each other and were buried on the same day at Overstrand church where there are tablets to all of them. It was the second time in her life that she has buried 2 of her children together. Grandpapa Buxton (*the "Liberator" of the Slaves*) whom I never saw, died only 15 days after my Father and Mother were married and they were called back from their wedding journey in Devonshire because he was so very ill, he was 58 years old, and died on the 19th of February 1845.

Sunday, Sept 20   In the evening some of us went to the Reading at Cliff House. We were there rather too soon, so we all sung a hymn together first, Prissy playing without her notes. It was entirely a family party, 33 in all. We had an interesting reading but it was not so easy for the boys to understand as the one last Sunday, as it was about the deep river in Ezekiel, but Cousin Edward explained it extremely well, and the boys were very attentive, finding out the texts and answering the questions so nicely.

Northrepps looks exquisite now, the Verginian creepers in the front have begun to turn red, and it looks most pretty buried in the trees,   The parrots and cockatoos are charming, there are 33 alltogether, two especially are the favourites they are most splendid leadbeaters, with pink wings & breasts, They are quite tame and only one can fly the other has been pinioned but they are so delicate that they have to be taken in at night, they were given by a Mr. Hibbert to my Grandmother because his gamekeeper shot two of hers by mistake. I believe they cost over £10. All the others come to our window, and we feed them with bread & butter. I am sleeping in the grey room which looks over the back yard & often 2 or 3 come at once while I am dressing. The old amazon talking parrot was the original of them all, he was given about 15 years ago to Aunt Chenda, she had him turned out in the garden and ever since that there have been a great many, he can talk splendidly and when I was a very little girl, Jay used to take us out in the wood, and he learnt to say "Come along little Totty" from hearing her constantly saying it.

Friday, Sept 25   Went to the last reading at Colne house, and heard that poor Mrs. Fitch has another relapse of the fever and is sinking fast all the little children came up to spend the day, there are 11 of them altogether.

My Father and Sarah Maria came home yesterday at 10.30, & brought down the big cockatoo Esau from Leytonstone. We put him out in the drawing-room garden this morning, and it was rediculus to see the welcome all the others gave him, the green parrots began to whistle on the trees, the little white cockatoos flew round him screaming as loud as they could and he himself sat on the back of a chair in the greatest excitement shrieking with all his might, & putting his crest, his feathers & his wings up, so that there was such a deafening noise we could not hear ourselves speak. He is about 5 times the size of the little cockatoos here, and would be very handsome if he were white but he is very dirty.

Saturday, Sept 26   This evening we got the sad news of poor Mrs Fitch's death, she died between 3 & 4 o'clock, and was quite conscious all the time, when she knew she was dying she fixed that her girls should not go into very deep mourning, just what they should wear at the funeral and what the baby should wear at its christening. She took leave of all her children in the morning and then lay without pain gradually sinking till the afternoon, when she died.

Saturday, Oct 4, 1863   This morning Fowell, Victoria, Uncle & Aunt Charles, my Father, Doctor Pagenstecker, the three boys, Isabel and myself went to Sheringham with a Mr King a geologist, to study the cliffs. We had luncheon in one of the fields and then walked along the shore to Runton, while he explained the different strata and rocks; at Runton Aunt and Uncle Charles, Isabel, Taf and I drove home in Uncle C's break, and on our way home we were turned over, I was never upset before in my life. We came to a very narrow part of the road where there was a cart standing, Isa called out that there was not room to pass, Aunt Emily said there was, so we tried at it, & one side of the break went high up on the hedge, and it fell right over, happily we just cleared the cart, we were none hurt, Aunt had a knock on her face which made her nose bleed and Isa twisted her arm a little but that was all. Our first feeling on seeing one side of the break go up the hedge was that we should be righted in a minute, our next was of momentary despair and in another second we were all lying on the ground, it was dreadful when the wheels went up the bank to know we must go over and we could not help ourselves. We all scrambled up as quick as we could, Alfred was on the box and was thrown right over the coachman. The horses behaved wonderfully they did not attempt to move an inche, but stood perfectly still. I ran to their heads directly and then a quantity of Runton people came to see what had happened, they helped to get the break up again but it was very difficult, as one of the horses had it foot entangled in the harness, but we were soon again on our way home and they were very interested to hear our story. It was indeed a mercy we were not hurt more.

My father went to Poles, to Mrs. Hanbury's furneral on Thursday. Each gentleman who was related had a large scarf of crape and those who were not, of silk. Papa had a crape one as he was related. . . .

Tuesday, Oct 14   An earthquake was felt all over England last Wednesday night. The daily papers have been full of it. It was at 3 o'clock in the morning. It was like a great beast lifting up the bed. There have been many letters written to the Times about it, & it seems quite to have alarmed some people.

6 of the poor little Fitches have the scarlet fever, happily it is very slight, but Mr. Fitch feels it a great trial.

There are now 8 little children in the house, Emily, Janet, Barclay, Effie, Nellie, Mary, Chenda and Sybil, they are such a really nice little party. Sometimes my Father has them all in his room to help him dress, and a fine noise they can make if they like.

Saturday, Oct 17, Today a large party of us drove to see the curious old church at Eccles. Eccles is about 2 miles from Hapsburgh, the old church was built about the fourteenth century, probably some way from the sea, it was after that gradually covered with sand and as that sand by degrees got blown off it again the body of the church also went away, how we do not know whether the weight of the sand brought it down or the sea washed it a way after it was uncovered, but the tower still stands on the shore at the bottom of the sandy cliffs, and the outline of ruins 3 or 4 feeet out above the sand is all that is left of the body.   It was curious to find near the church

87

the remains of the walls of old cottages, just the outline of their walls appearing above the sand, & old pieces of wood &c we also found. We could not find out whether it was in the decorated or perpendicular style of architecture because there was no tracery left, but it is curiously built the lower part of the tower being quite round and the upper part was of seven sides, with three windows, and we could see the remains of the battlements at the top of the tower. It is said that when the church was all covered with sand except just the top of the tower the people used to bury their friends at the steeple that being as they supposed the nearest place to consecrated ground, they were layed with their feet inside the tower and their heads out.

Sunday, Oct 18   Cromer church is not yet finished, none of the pews are in, only there are a quantity of forms which we all sit in. The church is always quite full. The Galeries are both pulled down, & all the new windows in, altogether it looks very nice. The worst of it is there is such an echo in it, each word the clergyman says is echoed by the other side which makes it very difficult to understand.

Wednesday, Oct 21   The three boys looked so pretty sailing their ships on the pond in the padock. My Father has given Arthur a beauty, & Geof & Taf have one to. They brought them up today to show them to my Grandmother. We all walked into the padock to see them. Granny is not able to walk far but she very much likes to come out and see all the children with their hoops and stilts in the garden.
The four babies, Emily, Barclay, Janey & Effie amused themselves & looked very pretty rocking in the boat in the Hall which they are very fond of, & never get tired of rocking in it though I am sure it would make me sea sick.

Tuesday, Oct 27   Pris & Isa were engaged to go out to dinner, but as Isa was so poorly I had to go instead, it was about the first time I had ever been out to dinner, we went to the Gurney Barclay's, there were 13 altogether & we came away at 9.15, before any one else. (*This was the family Ellen was to marry into.*)

Friday, Nov 27   We came from Northrepps to Leytonstone about a fortnight ago, & since then many things have happened. The 1st Sunday after we came home John Henry came home for his exeat it was so nice to have him dear boy again, also we have been to see Louisa at Brighton she was so

Teaching Effie to walk on stilts

Geof   Ted   Johnny   Janet   Arty Barclay   Lisa   my mother

Mending the ships in the school room. Silverstone

Maggie, Emma & Juliet Gurney, Emily, Janet, Effie & Barclay taking a run in the park with me before lessons. Ham House. Nov. 1868 —

happy in her school, but looking forward to the holidays which begin on the 18th of next month. Effie has learnt to talk and consequently chatters all day, & keeps all the nursery in order, making every one give way to her.

Dec 5, Saturday   It is her birthday today, her second birthday she was delighted with some penny toys & doll we gave her, she looked so lovely with a wreath of small white chrisantimums round her head which I had made for her, when she sees me she says "Ellen wait" & often comes up with me into my room, yesterday she told me "Daisy gone in garden, Hevvie go in garden," & immediately she went off to get her hat, she often talks about herself calling herself Hevvie instead of Effie.

Wednesday, Dec 16   A great event has happened in this family during the last week, and we are all very much excited about it, and that great event is, that Sarah Maria is going to be married, to Mr. Daniel Wilson, a clergyman at Mitcham Surrey, son of the celebrated Daniel Wilson, clergyman at Islington. He has four children so he is a widower. His first wife died nearly 2 years ago. He is such a very nice gentleman, I have seen him twice. Then there is another event which has happened, and that is that Uncle Barclay has actually bought a house and estate, we are all very pleased that they should have a nice house, but excessively sorry that they are going to live such a long way from us, I think it is about 2½ miles. It is Monkham's estate that he has been wishing to buy for a long time, at Woodford. I dare say they will get into it in about 9 months.

90

1864

January 25, 1864, Monday   And now I have not written my journal for a very long time, no, not since that very important day when Sarah Maria was engaged, which was on Sunday, Dec. 13. 1863. Never shall I forget how when she came to Leytonstone that morning she told me that "Someone had made her an offer and it was Mr. Daniel Wilson and he had four children.". That was all she said but that was quite enough to make me spend that Sunday in the greatest excitement, certainly it *was* the most exciting Sunday I ever spent, and especially as I did not go to church that day, and therefore had all the more time to think about it. She looked so pretty, more pretty than I ever saw her look before, in a black velvet mantle trimmed with grebe and purple bonnet. Well, since that time I have enjoyed myself very much it has been so pleasant to see them together evidently enjoying to be in one another's company, we were turned out of our little school room upstairs, and they came and sat there in the afternoon, with a bright fire and no candle and since then it has gone by the name of "The Lovers bower." But now comes the all important wedding day, it is to be next Thursday, the 28th of January 1864. On the 20th the three eldest boys, Johnney, Arty and Geof went to school to Cheam, the two latter for the first time in their lives, I dont think they minded it, but went off very happily.

Thursday, Jan 28
"On the 28th inst., at Wanstead, Daniel Frederic Wilson, vicar of Mitcham, to Sarah Maria, second daughter of the late Andrew Johnston, of Holton, Halesworth, Esq."

So the wedding is over and gone, and a very happy day of excitement is passed. It all went off very well indeed, it could not have gone off better. I got up early and wrote off to the boys at school, just to tell them that the wedding day had really come, and at 7.30 went downstairs to begin to make our wreaths and bouquets. Louisa, Janet and I are to be the bridesmaids from this house. I made Janet a lovely wreath of snowdrops and dark green pointed ivy leaves, which was very pretty, Lisa made herself a bouquet and Miss Smith made me a very pretty one principally of white flowers. Mr. Wilson (the Bridegroom) slept here last night, and after prayers he asked me for a white flower, so I picked out a most lovely camelia, much the

91

Consultation about the wedding dresses
Mother, Effie, Sarah Maria, Pris, Isa Lien & myself.
Christmas day. 1863.

most beautiful we had, and before we went to church pinned it into his button hole. At 9.30 I went up to dress, (as dressing to be a bridesmaid takes a long time) and was dressed first, Lucy did my hair beautifully and when I was ready the effect was like the picture I have here drawn with a long tulle veil nearly down to my feet. All the other bridesmaids were exactly alike except the two little girls who had white Llama frocks trimmed with swans down. . . .

Soon we heard that the Bride was coming so we all ran to the door, and there she was just getting out of the carriage. She was lovely, with a beautiful white Moree antique silk. . . . Then we all got into the carriages and drove off to Ham House, where we arranged the wedding breakfast. The greenhouse was in its most exquisite beauty, large trees of camelias quite white with blossoms and the whole place smelling deliciously. It was a most handsome luncheon with quantities of cold pheasants, patridges and chickens besides beautiful raised pies &c. Then came Jellies creams and all sorts of ices. There were two delicious pine apples grown at Rickerby. . . . When the Bride came down she was attired in a very handsome purple silk dress, and seak skin jacket and pretty white bonnett. Before they went away we had a few words of prayer & then in perfect silence, the Bride began to take leave of us all round, gradually the noise increased till she drove away

from the door with tears in her eyes. . . . I was not the least tired, I only wish another wedding were coming off tomorrow. Weddings are so charming.

Tuesday, Feb 2nd   We have heard several times from the Bride, they spent the first night at Dover, & went onto Paris for the Sunday, and now I suppose they are on the road to Rome, where they mean to stay a long time and not come home till the beginning of April.

*   *   *   *   *

November 15, 1964, Leytonstone   I have not written my journal for a very long time, the fact is I had so much to do & so much to say, that I was silly enough to leave it off, however now I mean to go on with it, & many things have happened since I last wrote. The birth and death of Aunt Barclay's sweet baby boy. The birth of our own darling baby, our delights at having a girl, our most pleasant journey to Scotland the most charming Autumn at Northrepps, The Barclays leaving their old house at Walthamstow for ever, and the birth of Sarah Maria's baby boy in the autumn. I think those are the principal events I can remember.

John Henry went to Repton at Easter, he is getting on so nicely there, and brought home a prize when he came home for the midsummer holidays, Arthur & Geof are most happy at Cheam, Arthur to his immense delight brought home a prize at mid-summer. Lisa left her school for good at midsummer, she was so happy there & was quite sorry to leave. Alfred went to school for the first time at the end of the midsummer holidays. He went to Mr. Hewitt at Rottingdean near Brighton, where there are 6 other family boys, Henry Gurney, Bertram and Sydney, Moritz, Carlos & Franky.

Barclay

Effie

But I must begin and write a better account of everything. Aunt Barclay's baby was born at Walthamstow, on the twenty-first of February 1864, they were very much dissapointed at having a boy, but he was a most sweet baby, a great pleasure to us all, he was a specially fine handsome baby.

Effie
Jan 2. 65

Effie

Effie in a runt
Jan 5. 65.

Our own baby was born on the twenty fourth of May,
My Mother was really ill for nearly a month before and Aunt Buxton was almost constantly with her, but after the birth of our baby she got on capitally, and has been extremely well ever since. The baby was born at five o'clock in the afternoon, Miss Smith, Taffy, Emily and I were sitting in the drawing room when Father came in to announce the news, we were keen to start off to Walthamstow to tell the Barclays as we were intensely delighted at having a girl, so we went off in the poneychair & found them in the garden. We were all very much excited about it, but Uncle Barclay was really jealous at our having another girl, I carried the baby in to the mother when it was about an hour old, the children were delighted, Janet was excessively pleased as she has been longing for a baby for a long time, and at last to her immense satisfaction one had really come. The baby was named "Ethel Mary", Ethel not after any body but because we wanted a new name. . . . So the baby grew & prospered, she was a delight to every one, we went to see her dressed every morning, and it was the greatest treat if the children might nurse her. . . .

The diary goes on in a desultory way until August 1865, but this brings us to where "Family Sketchbook a Hundred Years Ago" properly starts.